CONTEMPORARY

BLACKSMITHING

FOR BEGINNERS

Library of Congress Control Number 2024941515

Produced by BlueRed Press Ltd., 2026
Interior design by Insight Design Concepts Ltd.
Typeset in Menco
Photos by Pierce Valenzuela
on pages 4, 6, 7, 8, 14, 16, 19, 23, 26, 37
Photos by Keri Oberlyon on page 25 (top right)
ISBN: 978-0-7643-6919-3

Printed in China by Win Choi Printing & Packaging Co., Ltd

Published by Schiffer Publishing, Ltd.
4880 Lower Valley Road
Atglen, PA 19310
Phone: (610) 593-1777; Fax: (610) 593-2002
Email: Info@schifferbooks.com
Web: www.schifferbooks.com

CONTEMPORARY BLACKSMITHING FOR BEGINNERS

JOY FIRE

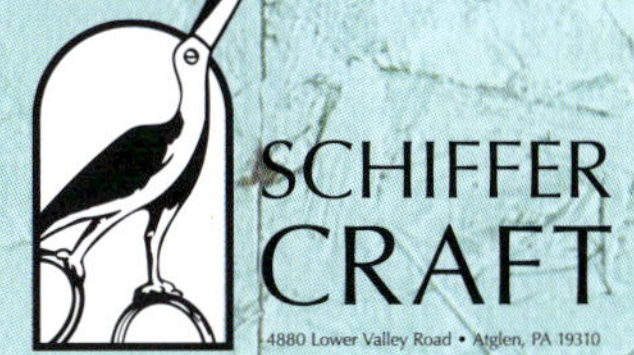

4880 Lower Valley Road • Atglen, PA 19310

CONTENTS

INTRODUCTION 7

THE BLACKSMITH'S SHOP 10
- The Forge 10
- The Anvil 11
- Hand Tools 13
- Power Tools 20
- Professional-Level Tools 21

HEALTH AND SAFETY 24
- What to Wear 24
- Ergonomics 26

METALLURGY 27
- Ferrous Metals 27
- Nonferrous Metals 28
- Heat Treatment 28

HOW TO FORGE 30
- Moving Your Body 30
- Moving The Metal 32

FINISHING METAL 34
- Cleaning 34
- Coloring 35
- Sealing 36

PROJECTS

TAPERS 38
1. Nail Hook 40
2. S Hook 48
3. Spoon 52

DECORATIVE ELEMENTS 60
1. Leaf Finial Key Hook 62
2. Scrolled Shepherds' Hooks 68
3. Simple Twist Bracelet or Handle 74
4. Reverse Twist Door Knocker 80
5. Ball End Finial: Choose Your Own Adventure 90

TOOLS 96
1. Chisel 98
2. Slot Punch 104
3. Round Punch 108
4. Drift 112
5. Monkey Tool 116

TOOL USE AND JOINERY 120
1. J Hook 122
2. Bottle Opener 128
3. Wall-Mounted Hook Set 134
4. Freestanding Double Hooks 142
5. Potted Plant Hanger 152

GLOSSARY OF TERMS 160

ACKNOWLEDGMENTS 160

Photo by Pierce Valenzuela

THE
INCLUSIVE
BLACKSMITH

Introduction

I first picked up a forging hammer in 2011, and I haven't set it down since. That same year I graduated with a bachelor's of Fine Art, and in 2022 I went back to school to receive a Master's in Fine Art. I have been an apprentice, foreman, teacher, artist, student, and small business owner/operator. Hammering hot metal has and continues to be a source of support, delight, and fulfillment in my life.

Because the craft of blacksmithing has been so valuable to me I want to share it with anyone and everyone else. I especially want to support those who might have a harder time entering this field, such as LGBTQ+ and BIPOC folks, women, disabled people, the neurodivergent, and those with less financial resources. To support this aim I volunteer with a nonprofit called the Society of Inclusive Blacksmiths, which offers resources and opportunities for more people to participate in blacksmithing. Find us at inclusiveblacksmiths.com!

Another way. I hope to support diversity and inclusivity in blacksmithing is the approach I take to teaching how to forge, which I have replicated in this book. I hope whoever reads this feels fully included in the craft and confident in their ability to participate in it.

joyfireblacksmith.com

ABOUT THIS BOOK

Blacksmithing is a huge subject with a long history, far more than can be covered in one book. This book is written with beginner blacksmiths in mind. This may mean you have taken a couple of classes or forged a few times on your own, or it may mean you have never picked up a hammer in your life. Whatever the case, you must have an enthusiasm for the idea of shaping hot metal with the skill of your hands, or you wouldn't be here!

I want to encourage that enthusiasm and help provide a solid foundation for your blacksmithing practice. My hope is that this text will enable you to skip some of the mistakes I made, so you can start strong and get further faster.

Remember, this is supposed to be fun. You will make mistakes, but then you'll get better and make fewer. The ability to see your improvement, and the satisfaction of doing something better than you did before, is truly a delight. I can't wait for you to experience it.

I have broken this book down into sections that build on each other. The first half of the book contains descriptions and illustrations of tools, safety concepts, and techniques. These chapters are not exhaustive but offer a place to start, providing a foundation you can build on.

Blacksmithing is visual and hands on, so it can be difficult to convey such physical concepts with just words. If you find yourself stuck on something you don't understand, don't get hung up on it; just continue reading. It is likely that as you start actually doing the forging, the writing will make more sense. Keep in mind that while my goal is to be as thoughtful and inclusive as possible, the information I am providing is based on my body, physicality, personal experiences, and mentality. Everyone is different and has their own needs. Feel free to adapt my ideas to suit your situation, while keeping in mind your own safety and the safety of others.

The second half of this book contains step-by-step guides on a series of projects. Every section includes more advanced techniques than the section before, but you can also pick and choose whatever inspires and excites you. Making each project your own and coming up with creative ideas and decisions is an important part of blacksmithing. I want this book to help you learn how to really *be* a blacksmith, not just how to follow directions to make the exact same thing as me. Your brain is the most important blacksmithing muscle you have, and you must build up your innovative ability at the same time as your physical techniques. With that in mind, I often mention changes you can make or other paths you can take. You should always feel free to make any change that you think will work or look better. If you struggle with a particular project, give yourself grace and space to learn. Keep coming back to it and approach it in different ways, and eventually it will come together. Remember, you can't get better at something if you stop trying.

Last, at the back of this book is a glossary of blacksmithing terms (see page 160). As you read through these projects, if you see a word you don't recognize, go look it up before you continue.

This book is written for you. You are welcome here, you belong here, and blacksmithing is all yours.

The Blacksmith's Shop

This section will introduce you to the basic tools necessary for a simple but effective shop space. You may not have or be able to afford all these tools right away, and they might not all be necessary for the type of work you want to do. However, they are common in blacksmithing spaces, and knowledge of what they are and how to use them will serve you well.

The Forge

Obviously one of the most important tools that every blacksmith needs is a forge. There are two main types of forges: ones that burn coal and ones that burn gas. Coal forges have been around since the beginning of blacksmithing and are still used in plenty of modern shops. However, there are several drawbacks to using coal. It can be difficult to purchase (depending on where you live), it is dirty in a way that can present health hazards, and it takes more skill to learn how to use effectively. Though coal is a viable option for some, this book will focus on gas forges.

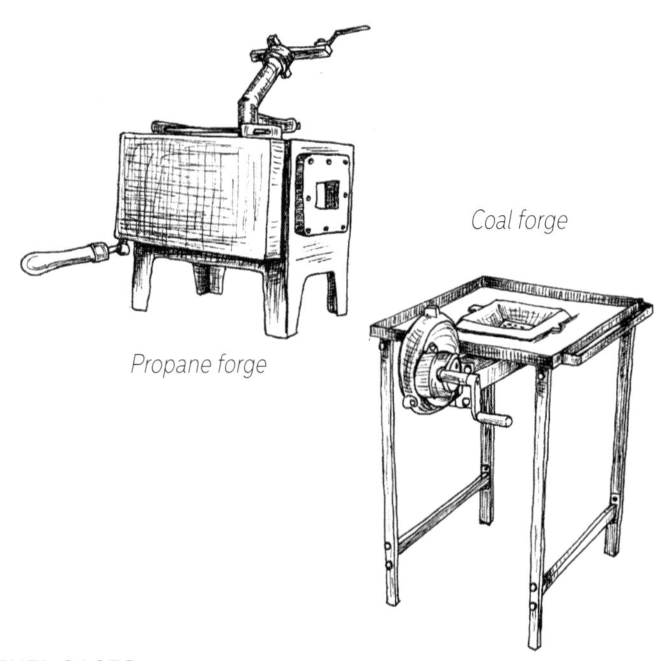

Coal forge

Propane forge

FUEL GASES

The most common gases used for forging are natural gas and propane.

Natural gas is what comes into houses for heating and cooking. A natural gas forge must be connected to a municipal gas line and is paid for as part of your utilities.

Propane is purchased in tanks of various sizes and is readily available at grocery stores, gas stations, or specialty gas suppliers for larger tanks. Propane is the fuel that will be most accessible to the most people, so we are going to narrow our discussion to propane forges.

BURNERS

There are two common kinds of burners for propane forges: venturi and forced air.

A venturi burner is a series of pipes and fittings pre-adjusted to draw in the correct ratio of air to gas for the gas to burn cleanly and efficiently. Gas is forced through a small orifice at the beginning of the burner pipe, where it is lit, mixes with oxygen, and exits the pipe as a neutral flame. Burners can be purchased or made at home cheaply, without the use of heavy industrial machinery. To build your own burner, search online to find something that will work for you.

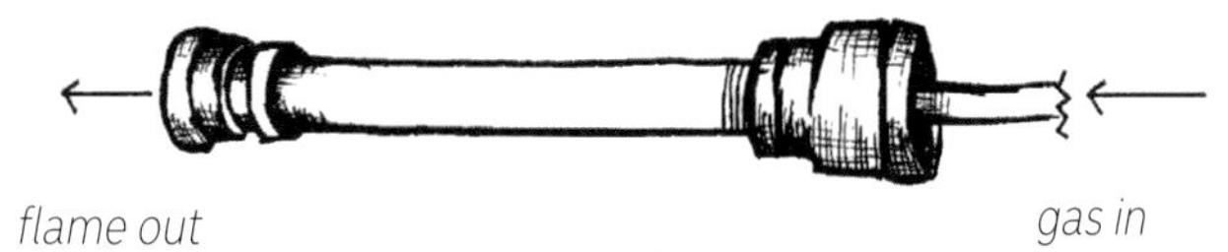

Venturi burner

Forced air burners are also a series of fittings and pipes of various sizes, but they are attached to a blower or fan. The addition of a blower requires the operator to balance the proper amount of air with the amount of gas in the burner. Too much air will blow the flame out, and too little will not burn efficiently, so the forge will not get hot enough. Controlling the amount of air from the fan that mixes with the gas can be done in several ways, usually with something called a butterfly valve, or a sliding valve.

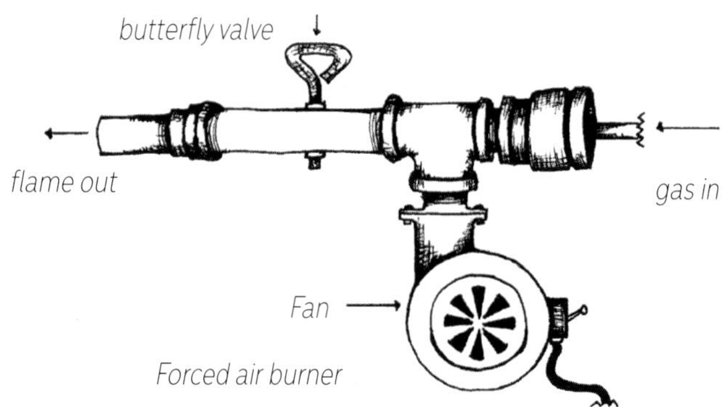

Forced air burner

FORGE CHAMBER

Once you've got a burner, you need a chamber for it to heat. You don't just want your metal to get hot; you want it *hot* hot. The key to achieving the proper heat is insulation, insulation, insulation. Two common types of insulation for forges are castable refractory and ceramic fiber blankets.

Castable refractory is like cement but won't crack in a high-temperature environment. It is very sturdy but takes longer to heat and is not as efficient an insulator as ceramic fiber.

Ceramic fiber blankets are extremely efficient but very delicate. They are also hazardous to your health because they contain silica particles, which can cause serious respiratory problems when inhaled and will irritate any skin they come in contact with. Safety procedures must be followed when handling this stuff—most importantly, wearing a respirator. The ideal forge will make use of both insulators, with the ceramic blanket fully covered by refractory cement on the inside and a metal shell on the outside.

My forge uses a single forced air burner. I use a blower purchased from an industrial supplier attached to a black pipe with a 2-inch (5cm) outside diameter (OD). This reduces to 1-inch (2.5cm) OD stainless steel with a ¾-inch (2cm) and ½-inch (1.3cm) OD pipe nested inside for the burner. I control the air that enters the system with a butterfly valve, which is a piece of sheet metal inside the end of one of the pipes attached to a handle on the outside of the pipe. I can turn this piece of metal perpendicular to the pipe walls to stop air flow, or parallel to the walls for maximum air flow.

The body of my forge is made of a castable refractory called Mizzou, covered by a ceramic fiber blanket and a sheet metal shell. It is a dome shape, with the burner entering at the top. It is modeled after the forges used by my friend Jeffrey Funk, who runs the New Agrarian School. His forges are the best I have used, but there are other great forge designs out there and forges you can purchase that will do the trick. Just be sure they can get that metal *hot* hot!

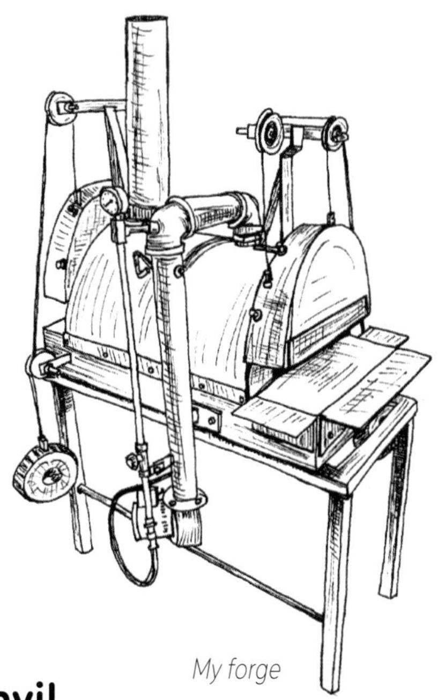
My forge

The Anvil

Anvils come in all shapes and sizes. Some of the earliest anvils and hammers were stone, and there are many blacksmiths around the world that simply use a large chunk of metal. We are going to be talking about a common type called a London Pattern anvil.

A London Pattern anvil has several main components: the face, table, heel, horn, and pritchel and hardy holes. The face is the main hammering surface, and the table is a step down from that and transitions into the horn—the pointy cylinder shape used to bend metal around. Often, the table is made of softer steel than the face, to act as a surface for using cutting tools. The pritchel and hardy holes pass through the heel, the thinnest part of the face, opposite the horn. We will discuss the uses of these parts in more depth later. The London Pattern is common, but so are other shapes, including

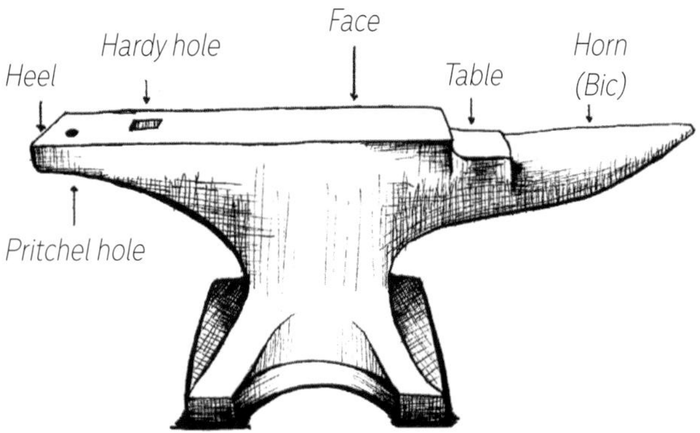

The London Pattern anvil

the Italian style or pig anvil. Most will have some of the same parts but in different places. If you have the chance to work on several anvils, you will probably develop a preference for one type. Beautiful pieces of work have been made for years with a simple block of scrap metal, so if that is all you have access to, don't be dismayed!

Anvils come in various sizes, measured by weight. If you have a small shop, you should probably look for a smaller anvil—one that you can pick up and move around on your own. You can make small work on a large anvil, but it is hard to make large work on a small anvil.

You can find new anvils at hardware stores for a fairly low price, but these are often not of the highest quality. Used anvils are great but can be hard to find. When evaluating a used anvil, check the face is flat, look for chips and gouges on the edges, and see if the horn has been dulled by use. Some defects can be repaired, but that gets into more complicated welding operations, which we will not cover here. The best anvil is one you can find, afford, set up, and actually use.

ANVIL STAND

Once you have an anvil, you have to mount it on something. Unless, of course, you choose to work on the ground, which is common in many parts of the world. Since I am familar with forging standing up however, that is what I will cover. Common mounts include a stump, a block of wood, and a metal stand with legs. It is important that the anvil is firmly attached to the stand so it does not wobble, the stand sits flat on the surface it is placed on, and it is heavy enough so it won't move as you are hammering. Any wobbling of anvil or stand means that some of your hammering energy will be wasted, making your blows less effective.

My anvil stand is a wooden box filled with sand. This is not common, but I love it. The sand makes my stand nice and heavy and makes sure that the anvil sits completely flat, without any wobble. This means the maximum amount of force from my hammering is going into the metal I am forging. It is not so heavy that I can't scoot it around the shop to change the orientation as needed. It also gives me extra area around the anvil to place my tools, and a wooden surface to hang other tools from. Again, the best stand for your anvil is one you can make or acquire that works for you.

ANVIL HEIGHT

The height of your anvil plays a vital role in your ability to forge effectively, but there is no one size fits all. Each person will have an optimal height, depending on how tall they are and the length of their arms. Placing your anvil at the right height will ensure that your hammer connects with the metal at the point in its swing where it has the most force behind it.

Imagine looking at a person from the side. They are holding a hammer and lift it above their head for a swing. Their arm is slightly bent. As they swing the hammer down, there is a point on the arc where the face of the hammer is parallel to the ground. That is where the face of the hammer should meet the metal to deliver the most effective force. Practice slowly swinging a hammer like this yourself to find out where that point is for you. No matter the height of your anvil, the most important thing to remember is not to slouch over the anvil face. We will talk more about your body position and forging ergonomics on pages 26 and 30, but for now keep in mind that you want to remain upright with good posture as you forge.

QUENCH BUCKET

This is a bucket, or other similar container, filled with water. Use this to cool your metal when you are finished forging and your tools as you use them. If you ever use tools made of alloy or tool steel (see page 27), you may make them brittle by quenching them in water, so be aware of what you are using. A plastic hardware store bucket will work, but something that can't be melted is better. A metal bucket, wooden barrel, aluminum beer keg, or something similar would be ideal.

POST VICE

This is similar to a benchtop vice, which you might be familiar with. A vice is a tool with two perpendicular jaws that can be tightened to hold something that you are working on. A benchtop vice is smaller and is fastened to a workbench. A post vice is larger and has a large leg or post that reaches the ground. The body of the vice can be fastened on the edge of a tableor other work surface to stand on its own. The post part of the vice, which goes all the way to the ground, makes it possible to use this vice as its own type of anvil. It can holder larger material than a benchtop vice and is much stronger.

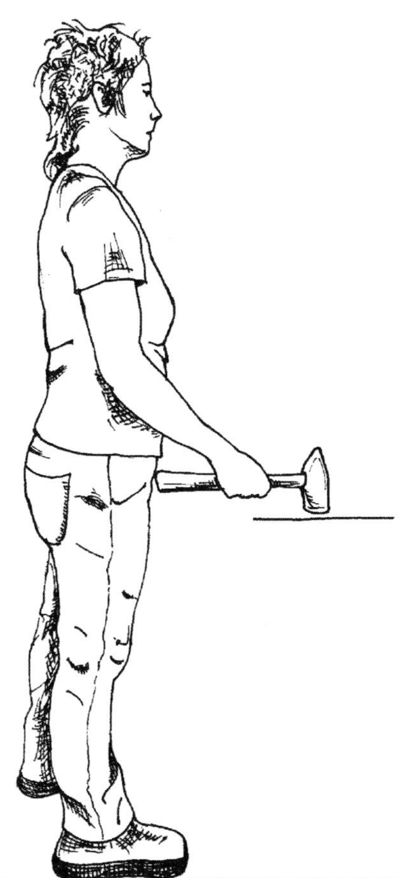

Finding anvil height

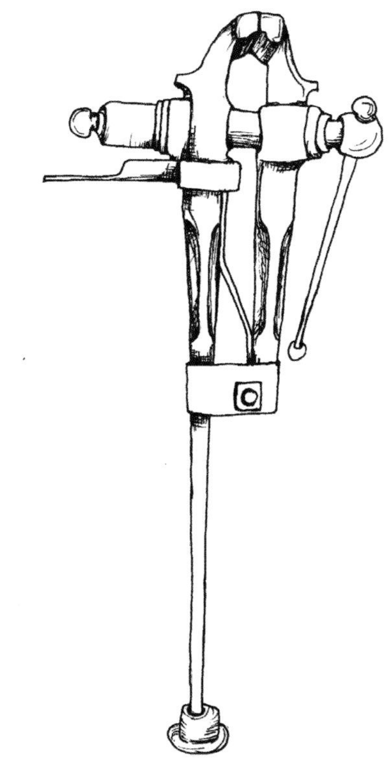

Post vice

Hand Tools

HAMMERS

Blacksmiths have many hammers for various uses, but generally one all-purpose hammer that is used most. A basic "quiver" of hammers should include this primary hammer, a smaller hammer for detail work, and a larger sledge-type hammer for heavy smashing. This should cover most of your needs, but you will undoubtedly acquire more hammers for specific uses as you progress.

When choosing your primary hammer, consider its weight and style. You do not want the heaviest hammer you can swing; you want the heaviest hammer you can swing accurately *for a long time*. When I began, I used a 3-pound (1.4kg) hammer, which I now consider too heavy. My current hammer is closer to 2 pounds (900 g), and I am happy with its effectiveness. It is a misconception that the heavier a hammer is, the more it will move metal; it is all about how it is swung. Technique is far more important than brute strength.

There are two parts to a hammer: the face side and the other side. Some people prefer a flat face, others a slightly rounded face, but the important aspect is that the face is not marred. Any marks on the face will be transferred to your workpiece.

There are many options for the shape of the other side as well—a rounded peen and cross peen being the most common. However, there are also angled cross peens, which are becoming increasingly popular. I use a square, flat-faced hammer with an angled cross peen made by my friend, Jeffrey Funk. The angled cross peen allows me to use the shape more effectively since my hand does not have to be directly over hot metal.

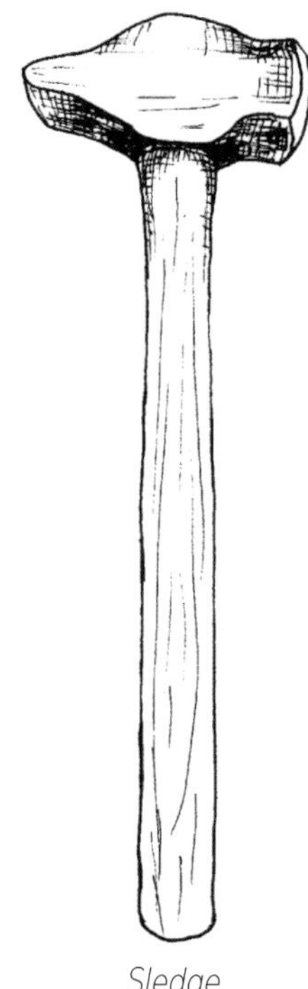

Sledge

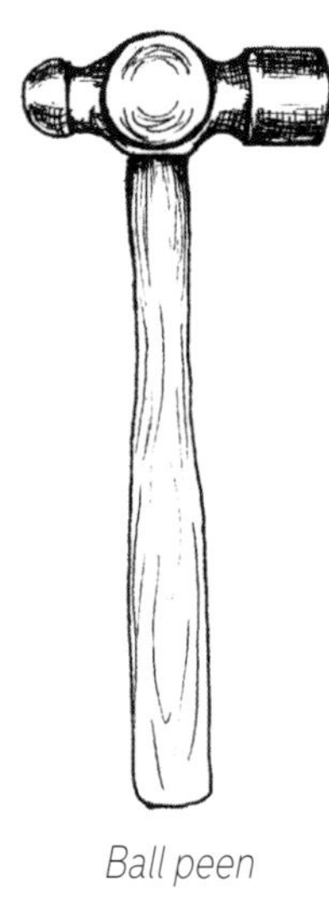

Ball peen

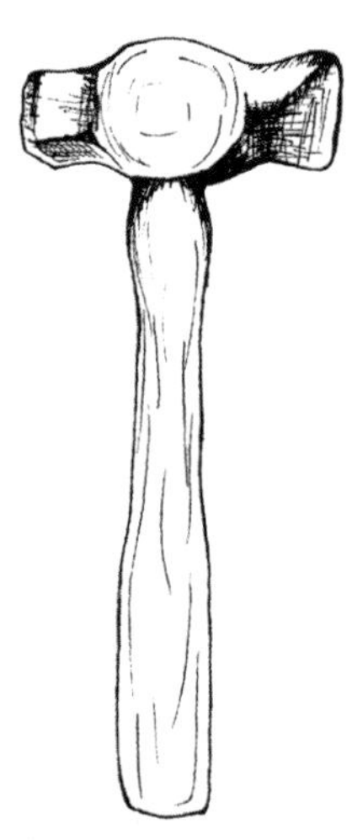

Angled cross peen

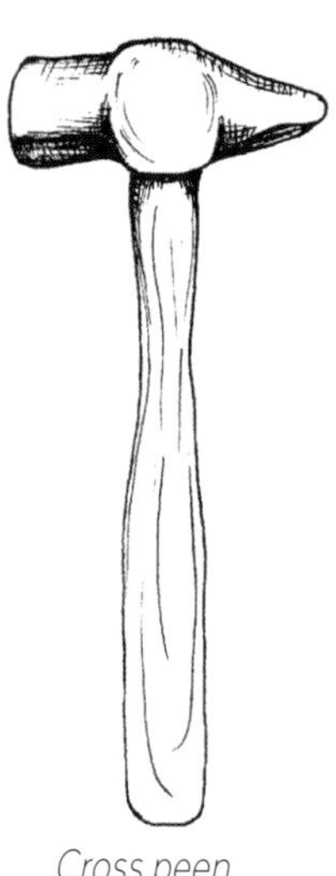

Cross peen

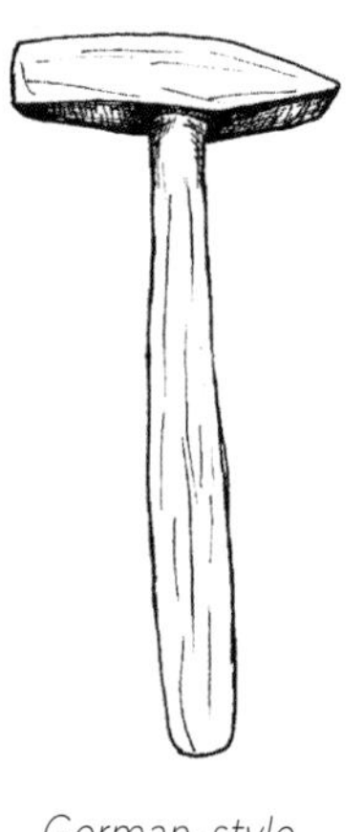

German-style jewelry hammer

PUNCHES AND DRIFTS

You will often need to put holes in metal. You could do this with a drill, of course, but blacksmiths have a more fun way. We use a hand tool called a punch, which is hammered into a piece of hot metal until it makes a hole. Then another larger piece of metal called a drift is driven through that hole to spread and stretch it into the desired size and shape. This minimizes the amount of material that is removed and allows for the familiar look of blacksmithing joinery, where the metal that is being pierced swells around the hole.

Punches are made of a high-carbon or tool steel (see page 27) that is tougher than your typical forging steel. There are two primary types of punches, which can be either handheld or handled: the slot punch has a flat rectangular end, and the round punch has a rounded end. Both are hammered into hot metal until they cut through it and remove a small piece called a "slug." You might think of them like a hole punch in paper. This process can take several heats for large material. The key to these tools' effectiveness is to keep the ends flat and the sides sharp. This means these tools often need to be resanded or "dressed."

Once the hole has been made, it generally needs to be stretched to the right size. This is done with a drift. With a round punch this may not be necessary; you can just use a punch that is the size of the hole you want, usually done in thinner material. However, without the drift you will not have the swelling around the hole that makes joinery so delightful. A drift can be various diameters and sizes—round, square, or even oval. Drifts can either be hammered into the metal and removed or, more typically, hammered all the way through the metal. This is where the pritchel hole of your anvil comes in handy. You can place the hole in your workpiece over the pritchel hole and then hammer your drift into that workpiece and through the pritchel hole.

Punches

Drifts

Punch and drifted hole

CHISELS

Chisels can be used to cut or simply mark metal. They are sharp at one end and flat or rounded at the end that is struck. As with punches, they are made of a more durable type of steel. The geometry of the cutting end can vary for different uses. A flat cutting end sharpened to a larger angle is usually used to hammer into cold steel to mark it. A more acute angle is usually used to cut through metal, and the shape of the end is usually not fully flat but, rather, somewhat rounded.

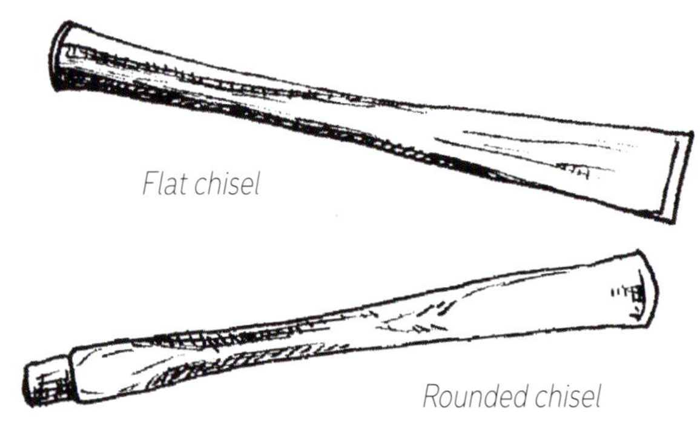

Flat chisel

Rounded chisel

HARDY TOOLS

There is a group of blacksmithing tools that can have very different uses, but all have a square shank designed to fit in the hardy hole of an anvil. These tools are grouped together as "hardy tools." One of the most common types of hardy tools is called a hot cut. This tool is sharpened like a chisel on the top. A piece of hot metal is placed on top of this tool and hammered into it until the piece of metal is cut through. There are many types of hardy tools for a variety of uses.

Hot cut

TONGS

There are many types of tongs that come in different sizes for different purposes. Most blacksmiths will have a wide range of tongs that have been collected or made over a long period of time. It is extremely important to use a pair of tongs that grip the material you are forging as firmly as possible. If you use ill-fitting tongs, you will not be able to properly control the piece you are trying to hit and will likely end up dropping it or burning yourself on it.

Tongs are generally made to hold a specific size of metal, usually measured by the metal's diameter or width. However, a pair of tongs can be adjusted by bending the reins (handles) to make the gripping ends tighter or looser. Blacksmiths often make their own specialty tongs for a specific use, but there are several standard shapes that you will see in almost any shop.

V-bit: The inside of the jaws of these tongs is a V shape. They hold square material sturdily by clamping on the corners. They can also effectively hold round material that is the same diameter of the width of the square material. Often, they have V-shaped notches in the tops and bottoms of the jaws, allowing material to be held perpendicular. These tongs are also sometimes called v bit bolt tongs, or just bolt tongs..

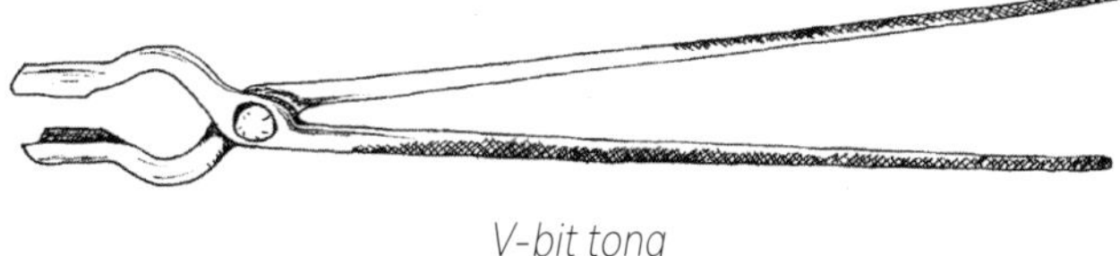

V-bit tong

Bolt: The jaws of these tongs are rounded instead of V shaped. They can hold round and square material and are better at holding flat material than V-bit tongs. The terms "V-bolt" and "bolt jaw" are sometimes used interchangeably, so you could just get one or the other.

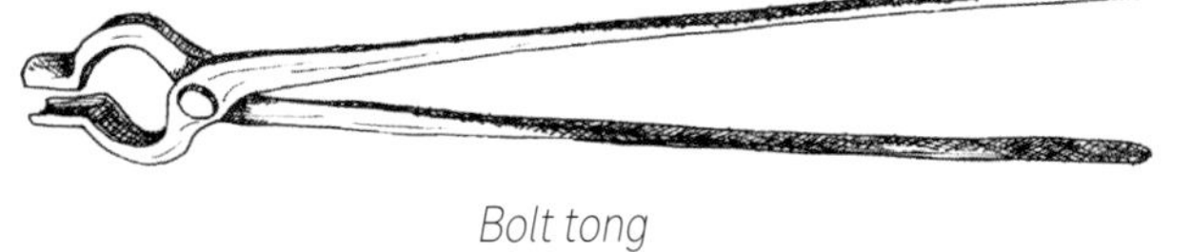

Bolt tong

Flat jaw: As the name suggests, the jaws of these tongs are flat. They can be used on a variety of sizes of flat material, but they are often not very effective at holding the metal still. Essentially these tongs just pinch the metal at a single point, allowing it to swivel side to side at that point as you are hammering. I mostly use these tongs to grab material, not to hold it as I am forging.

Flat jawed tong

Box jaw: These are effective at holding flat material, such as one might use for forging a knife. There are two primary configurations of these tongs. One is essentially a flat-jawed tong where one jaw has sides that prevent the metal from swiveling. In the other type, both jaws form a U shape, meant to grasp flat material on each side.

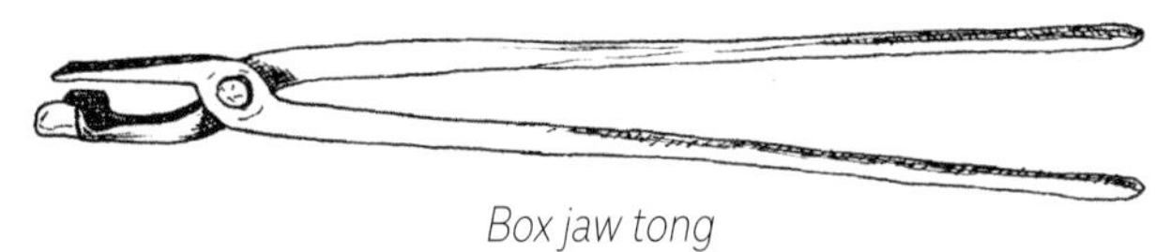

Box jaw tong

Pickup: There are many types of pickup tongs, some with flat jaws, some with thin curved jaws. Whatever the style, these tongs are used to pick up metal rather than hold it for forging. This comes in handier than you may think!

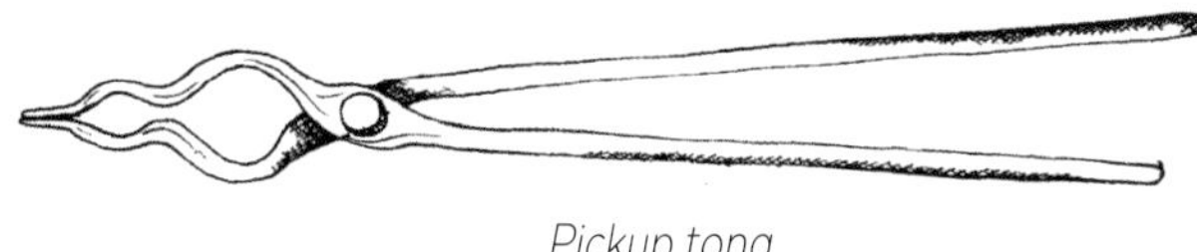

Pickup tong

Scrolling: Scrolling tongs have conical jaws. They are used for grasping and manipulating hot metal, often into a scroll shape. They are not used for holding metal for hammering.

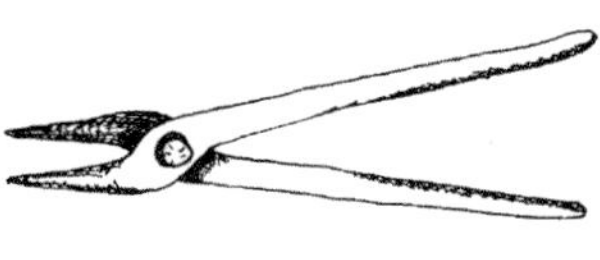

Scrolling tong

You do not need one of each of these tongs. My recommendation, if it is feasible, is to acquire several pairs of tongs of any type for common sizes of material, and perhaps one pair of scrolling or pickup tongs. A good start would be tongs sized to hold ¼, ⅜, or ½ inch (0.6, 1, or 1.3 cm), for example.

WIRE BRUSHES

A brush with wire bristles is used to clean the surface of your metal during and after forging. This knocks off what is known as "scale." Pieces of scale are hot and can pop off and burn you when you are forging. You can find brushes with a wooden handle with thin bristles at the end, like a toothbrush, or as a single metal block with thicker pieces of metal wire.

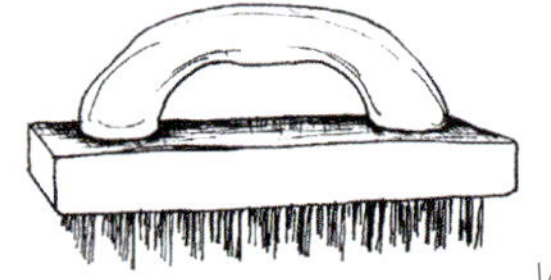

Wire brushes

FILES

Files shape or clean metal. They can be used to knock down sharp edges or, more intensely, to create lines or other decorative additions to metal. When using a file, you should think of the push stroke as the one that removes material from your workpiece, and the back stroke simply as the motion to get back into place. Trying to "cut" with both strokes will dull your file.

There are two types: hot and cold files. Hot files have larger teeth and are used on hot metal. Cold files have smaller, finer teeth and are used on cold metal. Files come in many shapes, from flat to half round to round. They are often sold without a handle, so one must be attached before they can be safely used. This can be as simple as drilling a hole in a golf ball and sticking it on the pointy end of the file, or as complicated as making your own wooden handle.

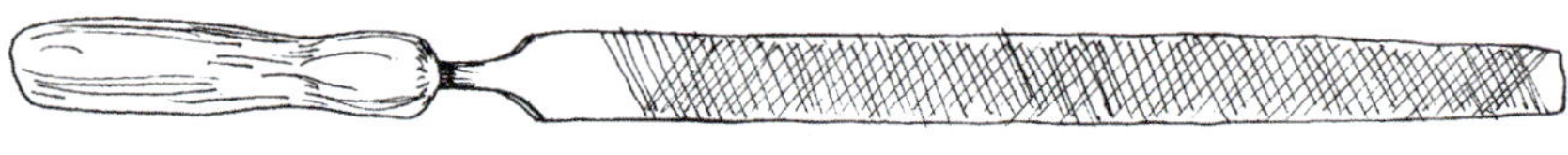
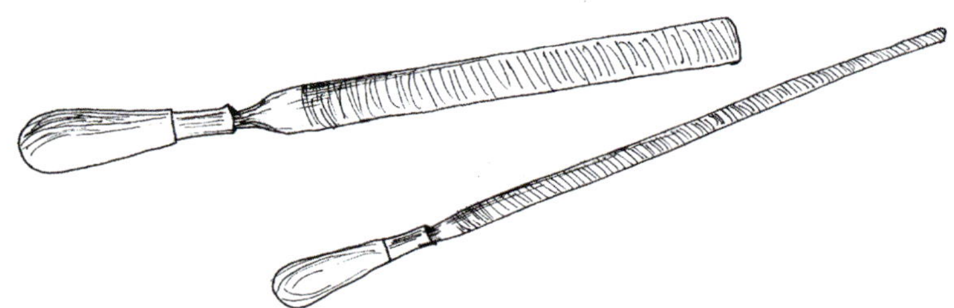

Files

Power Tools

ANGLE GRINDER

An angle grinder is extremely useful for metalworkers of any kind. It is a tool you hold that has an on/off switch and can receive various types of disks for different metal-shaping tasks. There are larger and smaller angle grinders, measured by the diameter of the disks they use. The most common size is 4½ inches (11 cm). Larger ones are much more difficult and dangerous to use. Common operations for using an angle grinder are cutting, grinding (removing larger amounts of metal), sanding, and wire brushing. These tools are hazardous to use, so you should be very cautious with them. Be sure to wear all your safety gear and keep all safety guards that come with the tool in place.

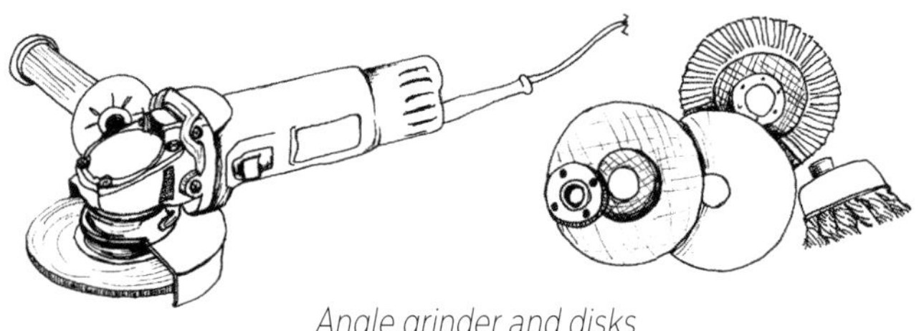

Angle grinder and disks

DRILLS

Drills are useful for putting holes in metal. Make sure you acquire drill bits that are meant to be used on metal, not wood. To hold and use the bits, you can buy a hand drill, a drill press, or both. A drill press is a larger tool with a chuck that holds the drill bit and a table that the material you are drilling is placed on. This ensures that you can drill a perpendicular hole. It is also much easier to use a large drill bit with a drill press because they have more torque. Handheld drills are great, too, and might be something you already have around.

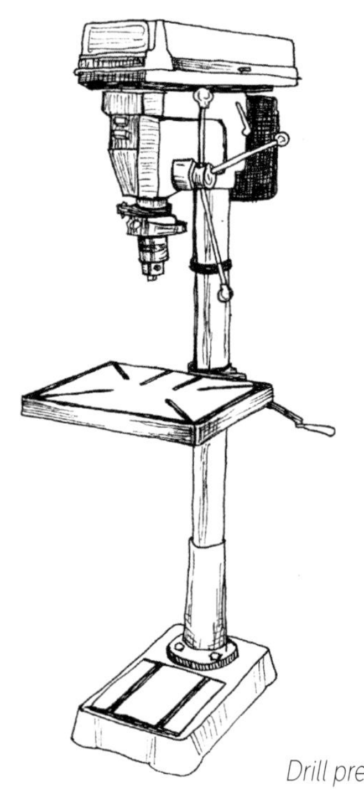

Drill press

SAWS

Chop saw

A chop saw is a tool with a large round blade that cuts material. There is an area where your material is clamped and a handle that is used to bring the spinning blade down into contact with your material. For metal, you can have an abrasive or a metal blade. An abrasive blade will be cheaper, but it throws hot sparks everywhere and is not as precise as a metal blade.

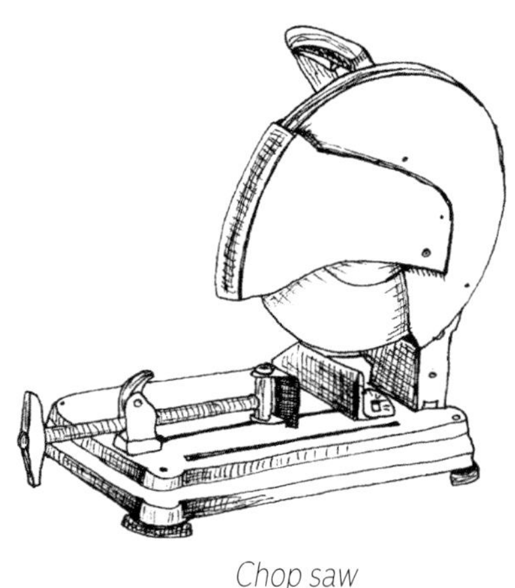

Chop saw

Band saw

An upright band saw is a large tool with the blade positioned perpendicular to a table that your material is placed on, while you feed it into the blade by hand. A portable band saw has a smaller blade and is, as the name suggests, easily portable. The material you are cutting is typically held via a clamp while you bring the saw blade to it. The blades in these saws are thin, flexible metal bands.

A horizontal or drop saw can come in various sizes. It will have some kind of clamping system to hold the material, with the blade horizontal above it. A mechanism will allow the blade to slowly drop until it contacts and saws through the material on its own.

In my shop, I have a portable bandsaw, also called a porta band, and a small drop saw. I recommend using a porta band for most of your cutting needs. It is quieter and less messy than a cut-off wheel on an angle grinder, and you will get a more precise cut with a thinner kerf. It also heats up the metal less, reducing the chance of burns.

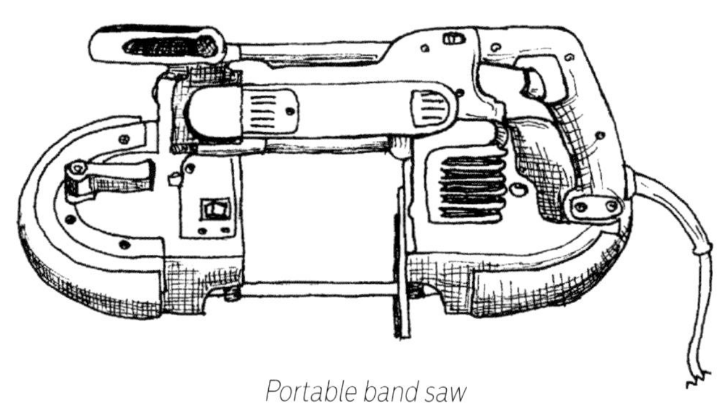

Portable band saw

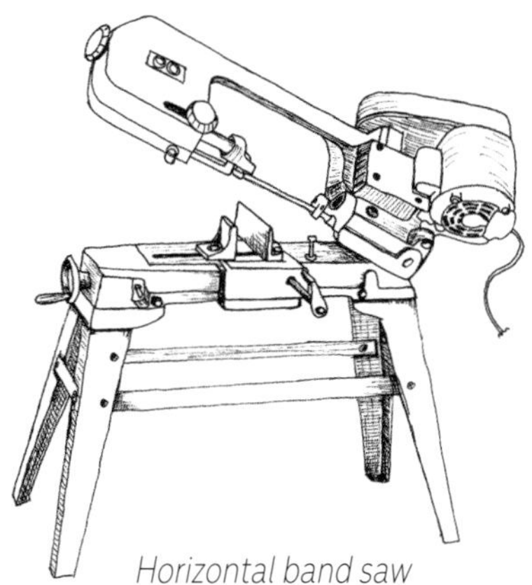

Horizontal band saw

Professional-Level Tools

While you almost certainly will not have access to these tools starting out, hopefully you will have the opportunity to use them at some point, so it is good to know a bit about them. Plus, big tools are just fun to talk about!

POWER HAMMER

The blacksmith's best friend! A power hammer does the hammering for you, using a non-human source of power. While there are many different designs, all power hammers have an anvil, a ram, and some way to operate the ram. Usually this is a foot lever, though in some large hammers that require two operators, there will be a handle instead. The anvil—the chunk of metal you place your hot metal on—And the ram, the part that hammers, will have interchangeable dies so you can adjust how the metal is being squished. Power hammers are designated by the weight of their ram, so a 25-pound (11kg) power hammer has a ram that weighs 25 pounds (11 kg). Even though this is small by power hammer standards, it is more than you can swing yourself!

There are many types of power hammers—from large to small, simple to complex—but all of them are a huge help to the modern smith. They are large, dangerous tools that have a definite learning curve. When you get the chance to use one, be sure to approach with humility and care, under supervision, and follow all safety precautions. My power hammer is a 25-pound (11kg) Little Giant, which is a mechanical hammer. It's small, but I'm grateful to have it!

HYDRAULIC PRESS

Similar to a power hammer, a hydraulic press helps you squish metal faster but differs in the way it does it. The two main types of press bodies are a C frame and H frame. A hydraulic system uses liquid to create pressure; you can have a small hydraulic system for something like a car jack, which does not require electricity. A hydraulic press used for forging is generally a larger floor-standing tool requiring 240-volt or three-phase power (more than your standard home/garage outlet).

Any press used for forging will have a surface for placing hot metal onto, with a cylinder that moves up and down slowly, operated by a hand or foot lever. It will be rated by how much pressure it can produce. For instance, I have a 16-ton press, meaning it can produce 16 tons of downward pressure. Most presses also have interchangeable dies, similar to a power hammer, to produce different results on the metal. These serious machines should be treated with respect; always follow safety precautions and work under supervision.

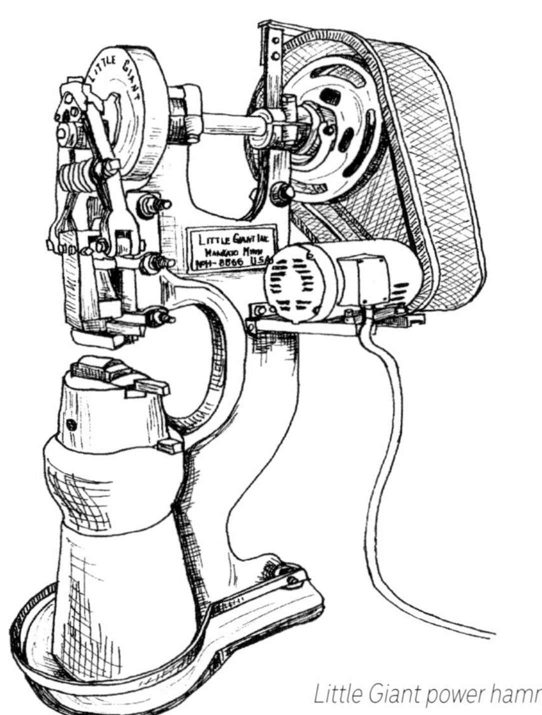

Little Giant power hammer

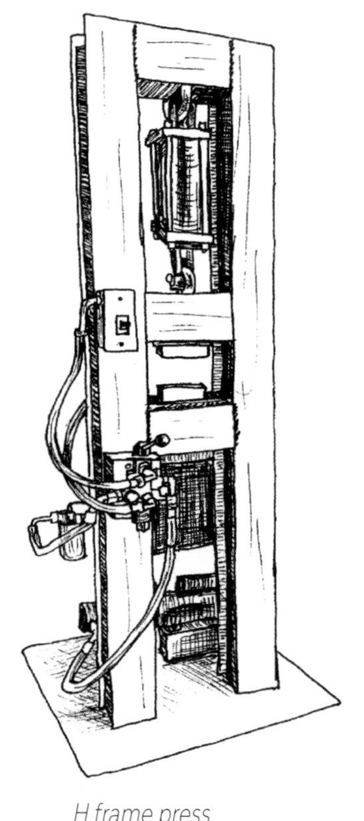

H frame press

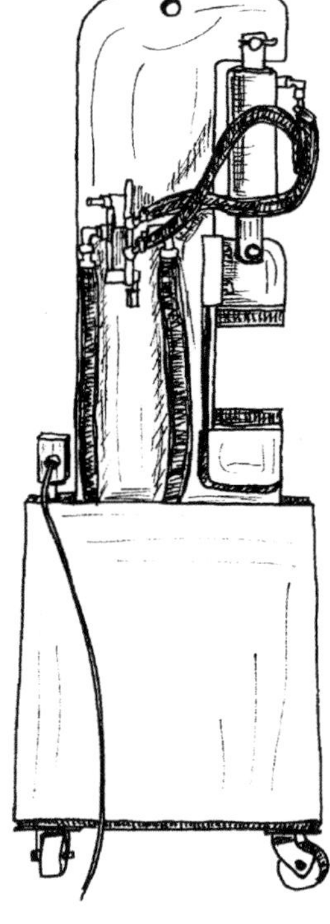

C frame press

FLY PRESS

A fly press is a fun and useful tool that many smiths like because it does not require electricity, is quiet, and is easy to make customized dies for. The principle is similar to a hydraulic press, but instead of a liquid pump system, it uses a large screw. This screw is operated by a handle that is spun or "thrown" to lower the screw and bring the die into contact with the metal. These presses range in size, but all are meant to be used on top of another surface like a workbench or table. Like hydraulic presses, fly presses are named according to the pressure they exert, meaning a number 10 press can exert 10 tons of pressure. These are industrial tools, so they should be treated with respect, but they do offer less consequential ways to hurt yourself than power hammers and hydraulic presses.

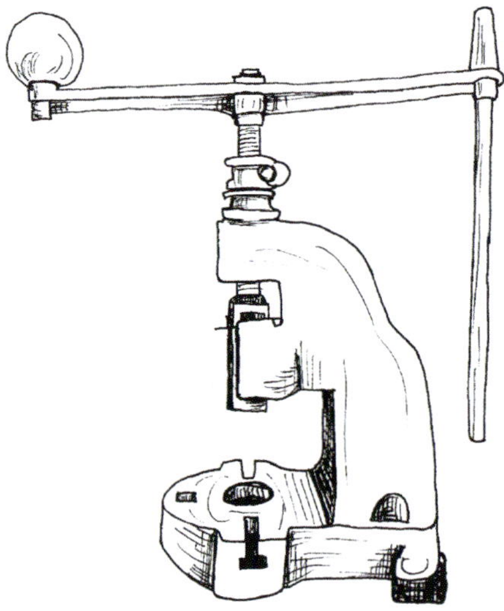

Fly press

OXYGEN OR FUEL GAS SYSTEM

While the main source of heat for a blacksmith is a forge, it is often useful to have a portable alternative. This is where an oxygen or fuel gas system comes in. Just like with propane, you can purchase cylinders full of oxygen and other fuel gases. The two most common fuels for a system like this are propane and acetylene.

Regulators are attached to the cylinders to control the flow of gases, which pass through hoses to a handheld torch where they are ignited. Different torch tips can be used for cutting, heating, welding, or brazing. These are useful and versatile systems but are also more expensive to acquire and take some time to learn to operate safely. Since you are working with flammable gases under pressure, there are real safety issues with these tools, so make sure you use them under supervision. I use acetylene for my fuel gas, which is more expensive than some but burns the hottest.

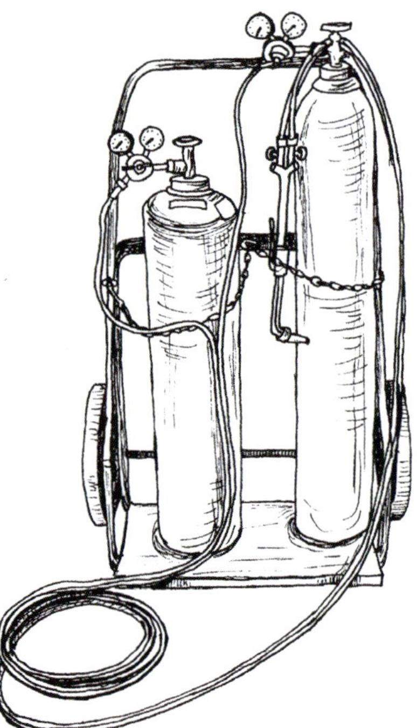

Oxy acetylene gas system

Health and Safety

Blacksmithing is a hazardous activity. That's part of what makes it fun! If you take proper precautions and use common sense, you can avoid serious harm and work happily and effectively for many years.

What to Wear

CLOTHING

All clothing for blacksmithing should be made of non-synthetic materials like cotton. You can purchase flame-resistant clothes, but unless these are required by a school or job, they are not strictly necessary for blacksmithing. Synthetic materials in contact with heat will melt to your skin, creating a worse burn. Natural fibers like cotton or hemp may catch on fire, but not as quickly or dramatically.

Clothing should be fairly loose, so anything hot that touches you is farther from your skin, but not so loose that it will catch on tools or easily come into contact with hot material. There are times when long sleeves are advantageous, but a cotton T-shirt and jeans are a safe place to start. Your footwear should be sturdy and comfortable; again, not anything synthetic—leather boots are preferred. Your pants should come down over your boots and should not be cuffed or have fringed hems. A cuff is a good place for hot metal to land, and the thin threads on fringed pants catch fire easily.

Example of safe clothing: cotton T-shirt; loose, uncuffed pants; leather boots. Other variations are possible and still safe —you don't have to dress like me!

PERSONAL PROTECTIVE EQUIPMENT (PPE)

Safety glasses, safety glasses, safety glasses! These are cheap and easy to purchase; there is no reason not to use them. If you use prescription lenses, you can find safety glasses that fit over them or get shatter-resistant lenses for your frames. You can even purchase side shields that clip onto your prescription glasses for extra protection. If you use an oxygen or fuel system, you will need shaded glasses to protect your eyes from the bright light of the flame. These lenses are rated by darkness; you should use at least a shade 5. You can also use a clear face shield that protects your whole face from sparks when sanding, grinding, or cutting.

Using an oxygen and acetylene system with extra eye and arm protection

Ear protection is just as necessary and as easy to find. You can use something that goes inside your ears, like squishy foam ear plugs, or earmuff-style hearing protection, which goes over your ears. Personally, I don't like the earmuff style because they make my head sweaty, but you can develop your own preferences. Hammering on an anvil usually isn't too loud, but power tools are. You don't have to wear ear protection all the time, but for sure put some on before you use power tools or do anything else that is loud.

My standard eye and ear protection

Breathing protection is another important part of PPE. Inhalation hazards are often more difficult to sense than hearing or eye hazards. This means you should be extra cautious and develop good habits to protect your lungs. There are two types of respirators I will cover: those that protect from particulates and those that protect from hazardous fumes or vapors.

Respirators that protect from particulates are simple and cheap. N-95 masks are one example, or a simple single-strap dust or painting mask, which should be easy to find at any hardware store. Even a cloth over your face will work in a pinch, though I would only recommend this as a last resort. Use these types of protection when you are exposed to small particles in the air; for example, if you are doing a lot of grinding or sanding.

A second, more expensive type of respirator is one that filters fumes. There are full-face types and even powered types, but for most blacksmithing uses, the half-mask type should be plenty. These are made of plastic or rubber that fits tightly over your mouth and nose and have interchangeable filters. They protect against vapors, acid, gases, dust, or welding fumes, but you must select the correct filter to suit the fumes or hazards you are encountering and change them periodically as they get dirty.

Half-face style respirator with P100 filters

Aprons are a common sight in many blacksmith shops, but they are not strictly required. Leather is the most common material, but you can find nonflammable cloth aprons too. Some aprons cover the chest down to the knees or lower; others are worn just around the waist. I recommend avoiding pockets below the waist because you don't want something hot to fall inside them. I only wear an apron when forge welding or working on something very large. Mine is the type that comes up over the shoulders, so it also protects my chest. If you have breasts, I recommend this type of apron.

An apron made from flame-resistant material with extra chest protection I added myself

With lots of hot and sharp items around a shop, gloves are always a good idea. You do not always have to wear them, but they are important to have around. Make sure to only use gloves made from nonflammable material. They should also be loose enough to fling off your hands if they catch on fire or get too hot. You can use welding gloves, leather gloves, Kevlar gloves, or something called "hot mill gloves," which are mainly cotton. Choose anything that is heat resistant and thick enough to protect your hand, but not so thick that you can't easily hold things.

A type of hot mill glove

When operating a machine with a guard, such as a pedestal grinder, you should not wear gloves, as that is a safety hazard. The glove could get caught in the guard and pull you and your hand into the spinning tool. I also very strongly recommend that you do not wear a glove on your hammer hand, but only on the hand holding your tongs or other tools. The reason for this is that you will have to overgrip to hold your hammer tight enough, which will tire your muscles quickly and is bad for your wrist, and the friction between the glove and your hand will create more blisters. You will probably get some blisters at the beginning; to deal with them, I recommend using a cloth-type medical tape to wrap the area until it heals. I mainly only wear a glove on my non-hammering hand when I am using tools on hot metal. Whether you wear gloves or not, you are almost guaranteed to get small burns on your hands from popping scale, but as you improve you will do this and it will affect you less.

It is also a good idea to have a box of rubber gloves handy for handling chemicals, which you might use for patinas and finishing.

Ergonomics

This last health and safety consideration isn't something you put on but, rather, how you use your body itself. Your body is your most important tool—you can't just buy a new one if you break it! I am not any kind of trained authority on kinesiology, biomechanics, or anything like that. The following is simply practical advice based on my years of experience. It is also specific to my body, so by all means, adjust as needed to fit your own body's requirements and needs. On page 30, there is a more specific discussion on moving your body to effectively move hot metal, but here are the basics.

Lift with your legs, not with your back. Imagine lifting an anvil off the ground. If you stand over it with straight legs and bend down to lift it, your back is the only part that is working. If you squat down, wrap your arms around the anvil, and straighten your legs to stand up, you are using your legs, back, core, and arms at the same time. Using more muscle groups means less strain on any one muscle.

Anvils aren't the only heavy things you'll need to move around, but whatever you are doing, the same principles apply. Be thoughtful and aware as you work and move around your shop. In general, keep your center of gravity low, keep your back straight, engage your core, and keep your shoulders down your back. If you take the time to set yourself and your space up and plan your moves, you will be surprised at what you can accomplish, regardless of your body size, type, or physical divergences.

Metallurgy

Metallurgy is the science and technology of metals; how they are made, what they are made of, and their physical qualities. This is a broad technical subject, so we will be covering just the basics that will help you to become a well-informed blacksmith.

There are two main groups of metals: ferrous and nonferrous. To keep it simple, ferrous metals contain iron and are usually magnetic; nonferrous metals do not contain iron and are not magnetic. There are four families of ferrous metals we will be discussing: carbon steels, alloy steels, stainless steels, and tool steels.

Ferrous Metals

CARBON STEELS

Modern steel is a combination of iron and carbon. Different percentages of carbon content divide carbon steels into three categories: low carbon, also called mild steel (less than 0.25% carbon); medium carbon (0.25%–0.5% carbon); and high carbon (0.5%–1.25% carbon). These percentages are general and can differ from place to place. The higher the carbon content, the tougher the steel but the more brittle. The vast majority of what you will forge is low carbon, your basic "run-of-the-mill" steel. High-carbon steel is hardenable, meaning you can treat it in certain ways to keep it harder, usually for making tools. It can be slightly more difficult to forge, both because it will not be as squishy and because it will be more prone to developing cracks if not forged correctly. Overall, anything in the carbon steel family is going to be cheaper and easier to work with than the following steels.

Various standard stock pieces of low-carbon steel

Alloy steels have larger percentages of other alloying elements, such as magnesium, silicone, nickel, and manganese. Each recipe makes a steel with different desirable qualities: easier to weld, higher heat resistance, corrosion resistance, tensile strength, and so on. They are divided into general categories of low to high alloying elements. These steels are trickier to work with because they are more complex. The more alloying elements, the more challenging they are. There may be certain temperatures that they must be forged at, held at a certain heat for a specific amount of time, cooled a certain way and at a specific rate, etc. If you ever work with an alloy steel, look up its properties and find the directions for the best way to work with it.

STAINLESS STEELS

This is a more specific type of alloy steel that gets its own category. This family all contains a base amount of the alloying element chromium, which makes them resistant to corrosion (hence the name "stainless"). Stainless steels can be forged, but again they must be treated in certain ways to maintain their corrosion-resistant properties. As with other alloy steels, you would need to do some research on how to work with these materials.

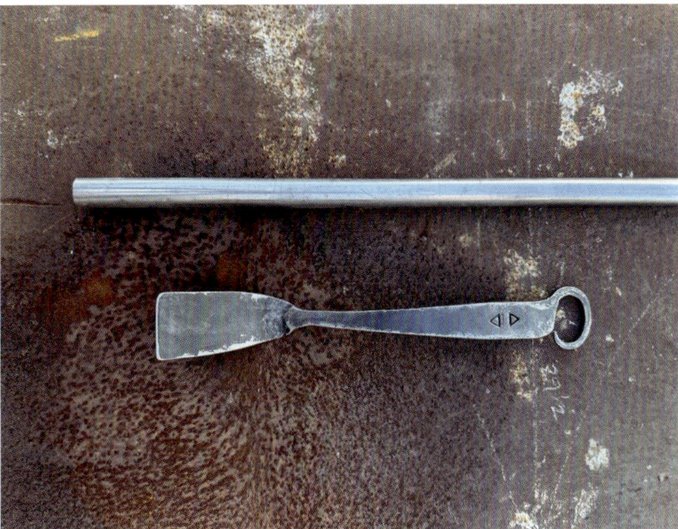

Forged and unforged stainless steel

TOOL STEELS

Tool steels do not have the same percentages of chromium as stainless steels, but they contain higher percentages of alloying materials, which necessitates moving them to their own family. As the name suggests, these steels are often used for making tools. Usually, a higher carbon or simpler alloy will be plenty for the kinds of tools a blacksmith needs. As with the other alloys, these types of steels—with names such as O1, H13, and D2—have specific directions for how to work with them.

Nonferrous Metals

Blacksmiths get their name from the fact that they work steel (or iron in the old days) that is black in color (a silversmith works silver, a goldsmith works gold). Any metals that do not contain iron are nonferrous, but blacksmiths certainly can work with these as well.

Aluminum, bronze, and copper are three examples of common nonferrous metals that blacksmiths use. Each of these has its own qualities, but they are all different to work with than steel. Aluminum, for example, does not change color when heated and melts at around 1,000°F (540°C), so it can be very difficult to find the right temperature range at which to forge it. Both bronze and copper also melt at low temperatures, but higher than aluminum. These metals can all be worked cold, but they will harden as they are worked and need to be heated and rapidly cooled to anneal (soften) them—the opposite of steel.

Examples of nonferrous metal, from top to bottom: brass, bronze, copper, aluminium

Heat Treatment

Ferrous metals are hardened by heating them to the right temperature, then cooling them quickly by Quenching in water, oil, or another special formulated liquid.. Water cools faster and oil cools slower; different metals require different quenching liquid. Some tool steels are hardenable in air. Usually, the purpose of hardening ferrous metals is to make tools. The harder they are, the less prone they are to deforming when used, meaning they keep their working edges sharp for longer. However, hardening also increases brittleness, so heat treatment includes a process of hardening and annealing to find the balance of toughness and flexibility so the tool will not break. Heat treatment can be a complex process, and if you want to focus on making tools (including knives), there will be a lot more for you to learn. The following is a basic introduction to the concept and a simple process you can use to make the forging tools (see page 96).

Not all ferrous metals can be hardened enough to make a tool. A simple rule is that the higher the carbon content, the more hardenable the material. Hardenable metals include medium- to high-carbon steels, alloy steels, tool steels, and stainless steel. Since carbon steels are the cheapest to buy and easiest to work with, we will be using them in this book. You can buy medium- or high-carbon steels from your metal supplier, but blacksmiths often use scrap material such as coil springs, leaf springs, and used drill rod from the oil industry. I can't tell you exactly where to acquire such things, as it will vary from place to place. Connecting with other smiths in your area can be a good way to figure out your local resources. I live in Southern California, where there is a lot of oil drilling, so I can quite cheaply buy 30 feet (9 m) of ¾-inch-diameter (2cm) used drill rod from my metal supplier. I will use this for the tools in the "Projects" section (see page 96).

A preview of the tools you will make

Heat treatment occurs after you have forged your tool to shape. In order to harden your metal, it must be heated past the "transition temperature." Think of this as the temperature that is hot enough for the molecules in your metal to move around. Different steels have different precise transition temperatures. To keep things simple, you generally just need to get your steel to a nice bright orange, but it doesn't have to be *hot*hot. To be a little more precise, you can check it with a magnet: When it gets above the transition temperature, it will no longer be magnetic.

Once your metal is hot enough, quench it in water to cool it quickly. This freezes the grains of the metal in a pattern that is tougher than it was before. However, you don't want your tool to be brittle or it will crack. You need the working end—the part that contacts your hot metal—to be very hard, and the struck end—the end you hammer—to be softer, with a gradual change from one to the other. Some tool steels need to be hardened in oil instead of water, and some are air hardening, so you need to know what metal you are using. For general-purpose high-carbon steels, water will be just fine.

Controlled quenching of a round punch—one of the tools you will be making

Steel has varying levels of hardness at different temperatures, which are indicated by colors that are visible on clean steel, with the dark surface of scale removed when that steel is heated. Of course, these colors are extremely subjective; everyone's eyes see differently and the colors look different in various lighting. But the colors that are usually referred to (from hottest to coolest) are light blue, dark blue, purple, yellow brown, straw yellow, and gray. Generally, quenching at the straw yellow color will result in a harder steel.

Temper colors on a chisel. Note: the light and dark blue bands are very wide, while the purple and yellow brown are thin. The straw yellow is the last inch or so of the end. No gray is visible.

The following is a simple process for heat treating medium- to high-carbon steel. More detailed instructions will accompany the "Tools" chapter (see page 96).

PROCESS

Start with your tool forged and ground to shape, with the surface of the working end sanded for several inches to bright shiny metal. Heat this end to its transition temperature. Avoid heating the struck end as much as possible; just 2 inches (5 cm) or so of the working end should be in the forge. When it is up to temperature, take your

Removing the oxidation layer to see the temper colors

tool out and dip ½ inch (1.3 cm) or so in water. Using a heat-resistant abrasive, such as a grinding wheel or file, scrub off the thin oxidation layer to bright metal and watch the colors move down to the tip.

Once you see straw yellow reach the tip, dip it again and repeat the process. You will do this quickly at first, then it will take longer as the metal cools. Repeat this process at least three times or until the color stops drawing. Set the tool aside to cool on a neutral surface such as a fire brick. This should help you achieve an even transition in hardness from the sharp end to the struck end.

Heat-treated chisel, cooling on a fire brick

How to Forge

Here we finally are! Everything up to now has been prepping you for this point, so you can come to it ready and well informed. I am going to break this large subject up into two categories: moving your body and moving the metal.

Moving your Body

On page 26, we discussed the general ergonomics of moving around a shop; now we are going to get into the specifics of how to use your body for forging. But first, an important disclaimer. I am an able-bodied, neurotypical person of average height and an average-to-athletic build. My experiences and understanding of how to forge are based on these realities, and the following information cannot help but reflect that. However, if your body or brain is different than mine, that does not mean you cannot forge just as effectively! You will simply have to adjust these instructions to fit your own circumstances. Also, I do not have any kind of medical or kinesiological training, so if anything sounds like it might be potentially hazardous for you, please consult a professional.

Let's start with how to stand. Your feet should be as close to the anvil as possible. This is why you don't want too large of an anvil stand. You want to be right over the top of your metal to have as effective a swing as possible. I am right-handed, and I position my body with my right hip slightly closer to the anvil. This allows me to hold my material tight to my body with my left hand position it on the anvil face directly in front of me.

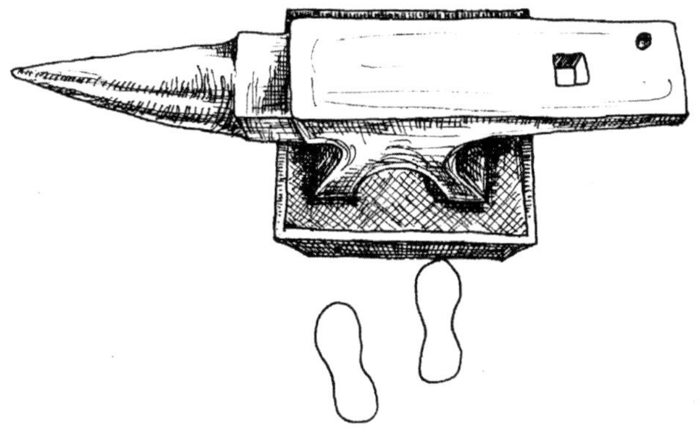

Foot position

Keep your knees loose—don't lock them. Stand up as straight as possible and keep your shoulder blades down your back. It is common to bend lower and lower as you forge to bring your face closer to your work. This is hazardous for two reasons. One, you don't want to hit yourself in the face with your hammer or have hot metal fly into your face. Two, a curved back with hunched shoulders will lead to a sore back and strained muscles. You can avoid these stress injuries by engaging your core and back and keeping your shoulders down away from your ears. If you are working on a low anvil, widen your stance to bring yourself lower. If you are working at a high anvil, stand on a sturdy platform to raise yourself up if you can. Whatever your situation, strive to keep your back straight and your core engaged.

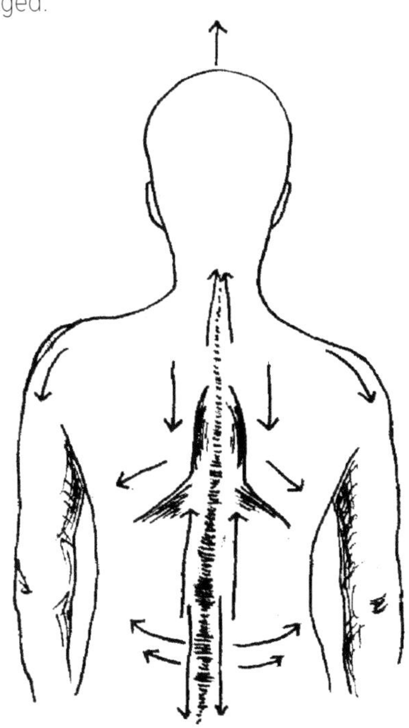

Core and back engaged, shoulders down

Your goal as you work is to use as little effort as possible so you can conserve energy and forge effectively for a long time. This means being as relaxed as possible and only using the muscles necessary for the action you are completing. The ability to isolate muscles is really useful, so, for example, you can use your arm and back to hammer on one side, while the muscles of your other arm are loose and relaxed as they hold your metal. Constantly be aware of your body and check in with yourself. I am always telling myself to relax my jaw and neck, bring my shoulders down my back to keep from hunching, and engage my back and core.

Hold your hammer in your dominant hand. The closer you hold it to your head, the more control you have; the farther away you hold it, the more force. Start holding closer to the head to develop your control first, then move your grip lower, as needed. Do not wrap your thumb over the top of the handle; it should be down to the side to avoid straining your thumb. Do not overgrip your hammer—this will tire your forearm and strain your wrist over time. When I bring my hammer down, it is very loose in my hand, and I can pretty much let go of the handle. Think of it as throwing your hammer through your metal and catching it on the rebound to lift for the next swing.

Swing your hammer by pivoting from your shoulder. You should not be hammering from your wrist or elbow, since there is very little power in that movement, and it will injure your joints over time. Your shoulder should not be shrugging up and down—the movement should be rotational. Imagine a circle with your shoulder at the center, with your elbow bent and your hammer in your hand. As you swing your hammer, it traces an arc of that circle. The arc starts with your hand raised and the hammer slightly above and behind your head; it ends when the hammer is brought down onto the metal.

Hammer arc

Your wrist should be loose so the hammer can hit the metal flat, with the face of the hammer perpendicular to the face of the anvil. Try not to scoop your hammer toward you at the end of your swing, which is very common at first. The power in your swing comes all the way from your feet, up your legs and back, and through your arm and into your hammer. This is why you want the muscles that you are not using to be loose, so the energy can travel through you without getting caught up. It is also simply more efficient, so your energy goes into hammering and is not wasted on tensing muscles that are not needed.

Another way to save energy is to make sure that when you are not actively hammering, you are not holding the hammer in the air. When it is not moving, your hammer should be resting on the face of the anvil, and the muscles in the arm holding it should be loose. If you watch blacksmiths work, you may notice a rhythm where the hammer occasionally bounces on the face of the anvil. This comes from the dropping and release of a hammer when it is not being swung. You shouldn't try to do this on purpose, but it may develop over time. When I forge, my goal is for my hammer to be swinging as long as it is in my hand. But sometimes I am slow, I am not sure exactly where or how I need to swing next, or my arm may just be getting tired. When that happens, I want the muscles in my arm to immediately relax, so I drop my hammer to the side of my work, the face of the hammer bouncing on the face of the anvil.

Your non-hammering hand will be holding the metal at the end, if it is cool enough, or in a pair of tongs. Either way, you want to use only the effort that is necessary. If you are using tongs, you will need to squeeze your hand enough to hold the metal tightly. If you tense your arm too much, you will tire yourself out and you will tend to move the metal around on the face of the anvil, causing you to chase it with your hammer. I keep my hand close to my body as much as possible to provide that arm with support. You do not want to hold your arm up too high or too low, but you want your metal to rest flat on the face of the anvil. That way, the force of your hammer goes into smooshing the metal instead of bending it. Of course, if your goal is to bend the metal, adjust your arm accordingly (more on that in the upcoming project instructions).

REALIGNMENT EXERCISE

Here is a brief exercise you can practice before you start forging, or anytime while you are working and need to reconnect and realign.

Stand with your feet flat on the ground, spread out your toes, and rock back and forth slightly from your toes to your heel until you find a comfortable balance. Make sure your knees are not locked. Your legs should feel strong but loose. Traveling up your legs, check in with your hips. Make sure you are not sticking out or clenching your butt or overtucking your tailbone. Engage your lower belly and back (this does not mean tightening, but pulling in and flattening out).

Next, imagine your spinal column is on a string, which is being pulled up out of the top of your head. Shrug your shoulders up toward your ears, then drop them down and bring them back. Let your arms hang loose at your sides. Loosen your neck and jaw. Take a breath in through your nose and let it out, feeling your feet grounded, core engaged, spine stretched, and shoulders down.

Moving the Metal

The first thing I want to impress on you is the importance of getting your metal hot. And when I say hot, I mean *hot* hot! When you are forging small material and working on simple shapes, you can get away with just hot metal, but if you want to take full advantage of metal's plasticity and you get into using larger material and moving masses around, you've got to have your metal *hot* hot. Heating your metal properly has a lot to do with your forge. If you are using a gas forge, you are limited by how well insulated it is. If you are burning coal, the problem usually is burning your metal rather than not having it hot enough. This book focuses on forging with gas, so let's start by assuming you have a good gas forge that is set up right and able to get nice and toasty, at least 2,000°F (1,093°C).

A gas forge will take a certain amount of time to get up to heat. How long depends on what material it is made of. Regardless of how long it takes, it is not helpful to put your metal into the forge before it is up to heat. This just brings the temperature of the forge down and is not good for the quality of the metal. You can tell when your forge is up to heat by looking at the color, since the interior of your forge will look different depending on the material it is made of. In general, it should all be glowing a bright white orange. As you use your forge, you will get to know it and will be able to tell when it is at its peak temperature.

Once you do put your metal in the forge, you have to exercise patience again by waiting until the metal itself is up to heat. Again, you will determine this by the color. The metal should look the same color or a little brighter than the interior of the forge. Most gas forges will not be able to get your metal too hot, but some can, so if you see your metal starting to throw off white sparks, it is time to pull it out and back off on the heat.

As soon as you pull your material out of the forge, it will start to cool. When you place the metal on the face of the anvil, it will cool even more, as the mass of the anvil absorbs the heat. So, while you don't want to be frantic, you do want to move with efficiency. Small material, while easier to move in general, can be more difficult to forge because it cools quickly. Regardless of what size of stock you are using, you should know what you will be doing with the metal before you pull it out, and have your tools close to hand so you can use them quickly.

Watch the color of the metal as you forge, and pay attention to how it feels under your hammer. As it cools, it becomes less malleable, and at a certain point it is not going to deform anymore—you will just be denting the surface. This is usually when your metal gets to a red color instead of a hot orange. You should stop hammering just before you get to the point where it is too cold. Put your metal back in the forge and heat it up again. You are going to complete your finished piece faster if you stop and reheat as needed, instead of continuing to hammer when your material is too cold. At the same time, however, you do want to reduce the overall number of heats that you have to take for each piece. Each time you heat the metal up, small amounts of iron flake off in the form of scale. Losing iron means losing mass, plus your material will eventually become brittle. As you get better and make the same pieces multiple times, you will become more efficient in your actions and will need fewer and fewer heats.

Think of your metal like clay. If you have a lump of clay in your hand and press your finger into it, you will dent the clay and it will squish out around that pressure. If you were to press the lump with your whole hand, it will squish and flatten in a different way. Metal reacts to pressure in a similar manner, as long as it is hot enough. Most of what you are doing as you forge is figuring out how and where to apply pressure to your metal to achieve the shape you want. Pressure is applied with your hammer, the surface of the anvil that you hammer on, and the various top and bottom tools, hardy tools, etc. that you have available to use.

FORGING TAPERS

To help you understand how metal moves, I will walk you through forging two tapers. These simple shapes are common in blacksmithing; you will be forging them in many of the upcoming projects.

A pointed taper consists of a piece of metal that comes to a point. It can be square, with four faces, or round. It can be made from square or round material, but round material must be forged into square first. A taper is forged by increasing the heaviness and amount of hits from the non-tapered end to the tapered end.

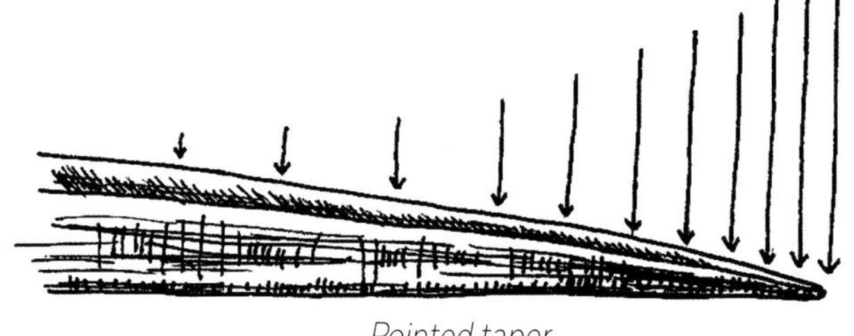

Pointed taper

Generally, it is easiest to begin at the non-tapered end—or wherever the taper will start—with light blows, and to modulate to increasingly heavier blows as you move toward the pointed end. Usually, the goal is to have a gradual taper, so the exact starting point should vary. Start this process, moving from light to heavy blows, on one face of the material, rotate it 90 degrees to the next face, repeat the hammering, and continue rotating. If your material is round, this process will shape it square. To get a rounded taper, simply take your square taper, place it with one corner up and one corner on the anvil (I call this "on the diamond"), and hammer that corner down. This will result in an octagon, which can be further rounded.

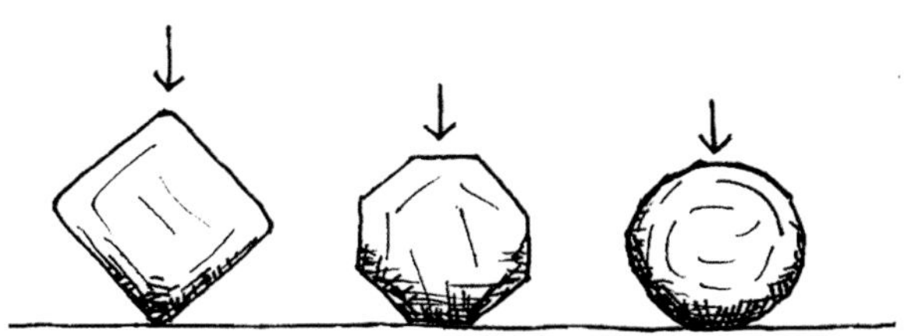

Forging square to round

A flat taper is one where only two faces of the material taper to a point. The "top" and "bottom" faces will either remain the same width as the stock material or be allowed to flare out wider, resulting in what is called a billed taper.

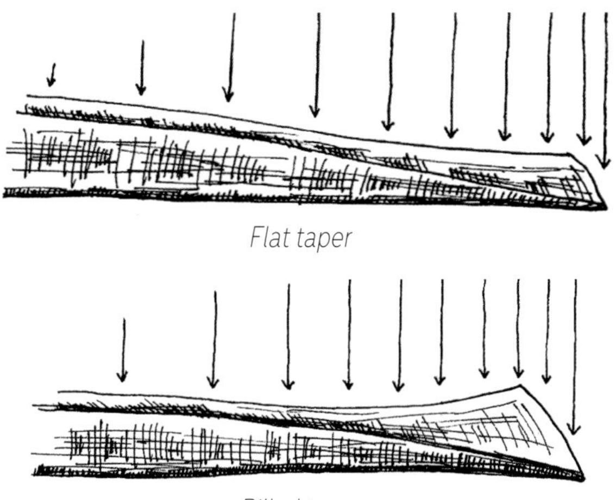

Flat taper

Billed taper

Process to achieve either of these tapers is similar to the pointed taper, with important changes. Instead of rotating your material 90 degrees after the first pass, rotate it a full 180 degrees and repeat the same steps. Do this until two faces come to a point and two faces are flat. Then place your metal so the flat faces are side to side on your anvil, and lightly hammer along the tapered faces to clean up the lines and keep them straight. If you want to keep your taper flat instead of billed, you will need to do this step sooner to keep the end from widening.

PLANNING

Part of being an effective blacksmith is designing and planning. The projects coming up in the next section are planned for you, but there are variations you can take as you improve your forging abilities. Obviously, you want to continue to forge after you finish these projects, so these design variations are practice for you to plan an entire project on your own. The larger and more complex your projects get, the more important planning will be. Of course, there is always room for change, since you might have a better idea or have a "happy accident" that you really like. I do like to have some play time at the anvil to let the metal guide me.

Start with a sketch. Don't worry about being clean, accurate, or to scale. My first sketches are really "sketchy," with lots of lines in all directions. This step is to define the shape and volume of what you will be making. Once you have your general idea in place, move on to a detailed drawing.

This step will take a lot longer. You will decide the measurements for every part of your piece, determine what size of stock material(s) to use, and determine the forging processes to get the shapes you want. I like to draw on vellum, which is like tracing paper but sturdier. That way, I can make traces of the body of an object and work out different variations without having to start from the beginning every time. It is also easy to erase and doesn't smudge as much as paper. You should be able to find something like this at an art supply store.

As part of the detailed drawing phase, or after it, making a three-dimensional model is often helpful. This kind of mockup of a project is called a maquette. As I said before, metal is quite like clay, so it can be extremely informative to use clay to make a specific shape or part of your project. This allows you to see what the shape will look like, and to think through how you will apply your tools to achieve it. Sometimes I will make parts out of clay just to figure out how to draw them. You can also use other material, such as wooden skewers and glue, to get a rough idea of how your project will feel in space. You can always make your model out of metal, just smaller and simpler than what the final version will be, which is helpful for testing patinas and finishes.

Sketching, drawing, and making maquettes are all helpful practices to engage in to improve yourself as a blacksmith, but we don't always do things the "right" way, do we? I am always impatient to get my hammer on metal, so I often skip steps or take shortcuts. Sometimes it works out; sometimes it doesn't. If this planning process doesn't work for you, then come up with your own. Remember that this is supposed to be fun. Give yourself freedom to play.

Finishing Metal

Each object you make takes time and effort, so it deserves the final step of being finished properly. There are whole books dedicated to the art of finishing metal, so feel free to explore if you find this interesting. For our purposes, we will go over the basic steps needed to bring your project to a completed state. "Finishing" in this case means cleaning off loose scale, possibly using a patina or stain, and finally sealing the metal to prevent rust. Let's go through each step.

Cleaned metal with no patina or finish applied

Darkening/aging patina with clear finish applied

Cleaning

You want to remove any loose scale or oxidation that might remain on your metal, and to ensure that the surface is uniform. As you are doing the initial forging, you should use your wire brush occasionally to remove scale as it forms. You can also do this with your completed object, and since it is cold you can be more thorough. Scale can also be removed by lightly hammering your object on your anvil. This pops loose scale off and helps planish, or smooth, the surface. Working by hand like this with something larger can be difficult, so you may want

Using a wire brush cup on an angle grinder

I often use a cup brush on my angle grinder, which you can buy in a light or coarse wire. You can also use a wire wheel on a pedestal grinder. However, either powered wire wheel option can be extremely dangerous, both because it can catch your metal and fling it back at you and because the wires of the brush fly off and can embed themselves in your skin. Delightful. It is a great idea to use extra PPE, like a face shield, sleeves, and gloves, when using a wire brush.

If you are using an angle grinder, it is also much safer to hold your material in a vice or have it clamped to a solid surface than to hold it in your hand. If you are using a pedestal grinder, it is only safe to wear gloves if there is no guard around the wheel. If there is a guard, gloves and even loose sleeves are a safety hazard. They can get caught on the wire wheel and pull you into it, catching you between the wheel and the guard for a worse injury. If you do not have or do not want to use a wire wheel, brushing by hand is just fine.

Wire-brushed objects

Another step to take after wire brushing is to scrub your piece thoroughly with a scouring pad or steel wool. There are various levels of aggressiveness with both products, from heavy duty to fine. I usually go with a medium duty, sometimes moving on to a lighter duty for extra polish. You can even do this in water to make sure that the dirt and scale are fully removed from the material. There are also various sandpapers that can be used wet, either in place of or after using a scouring pad. If you do use water, be sure to completely dry your piece off quickly once you are done.

You can decide if you want to go through each of these steps or if just a few are good enough for your project. Generally, the more effort you put into finishing your project, the better it looks. You have put a lot of effort into making this object and it deserves to be treated with care and respect.

Coloring

When your project is properly cleaned and polished, it will be a uniform silver/gray. This is perfectly acceptable and you could move right on to sealing it. Otherwise, you could explore altering the color with patinas, stains, or even paint.

PATINAS

Patinas are various chemical mixtures that interact with the surface of your metal to alter the color. Think of them as a faster and more controlled aging process. Some are formulated to interact only with specific metals; others are universal and are more in the realm of stains, which we will get to next. With a patina, you will not get one universal color; you may get more of a black or brown, but there will be a wonderful richness and variety in the tones. There are many recipes out there for patinas you can make yourself, or there are premade products you can buy. Either way, be aware that you are working with corrosive chemicals. Wear the proper PPE, like rubber gloves and safety glasses, and follow all the directions for safe use and disposal.

Close-up of an object with several layers of patina

STAINS

A stain is not a chemical reaction with the metal but a layer of color on its surface. Staining metal is just like staining wood or clothes. You can use a black or brown stain on metal to darken it, but you will not get the same color variation as with a patina. You can also use stains to achieve brighter and more vibrant colors, like red, green, and purple. Since steel is dark, it can be hard to see the effects of darker colored stains or to get bright colors with light stains. A yellow stain, for example, will look very different than a yellow paint. You can purchase premade metal stains or find recipes to make your own. Pay attention to all relevant safety precautions when using stains.

Examples of blue and green stain on carbon steel

PAINT

You can also paint your finished metal. It can be applied via a brush or a spray can, or you can take your piece to a professional. Be sure to get paint that is specifically for applying to metal. It is also a good idea to use a primer for a longer-lasting finish. If your piece will be outdoors, make sure to get a good UV-stable paint that will not fade or flake. If you are spraying paint, wear a proper respirator and, of course, glasses and gloves.

POWDER COAT

Another finishing process that is common for large outdoor objects is powder coating. With this process, a powder is sprayed on the metal, and the piece is then heated. The powder melts and coats the metal, providing a durable surface. It is possible to buy the tools to do small-scale powder coating yourself, but usually you would take your piece to a specialized shop.

Sealing

If your project is painted or powder coated, you are done—that is all the finishing it needs. But with patinas and stains, the metal must also be sealed against moisture to prevent rusting. You can also seal directly on raw metal. Below are some common sealing methods.

WAXES

There are recipes for homemade waxes made with a mixture of turpentine and beeswax, which are very traditional. Simple furniture wax, which is cheaper and easier to acquire, will work as well. There are also specific metal wax products available.

Whatever wax you use, the method is similar. Rub the wax on, let it soak in and harden for a bit, then buff it off. I like to apply wax when my metal is warm—either in the sun or warmed with a torch. It should not be hot enough to burn the wax—I still want to be able to hold it in my hand—but it should be warm enough so that the wax melts into any holes or joints. I like to apply wax with a rubber glove and buff it off with a cotton cloth. If you have a stain or patina on your piece, the wax will usually change how it looks, so test some scraps first to make sure you get a finish you like.

OILS

Oils work in a similar way to waxes. The difference is that they are liquid and may offer a less-robust finish. If you are making an object for cooking or wearing, food oils such as olive or coconut are recommended. There is a product commonly used for wood finishing called boiled linseed oil, and, of course, there are metal-specific oils available for purchase as well.

The application method is similar to wax, but the metal has less need to be heated and the curing or drying time will be longer. Again, oils will change the look of a patina or stained finish, so make sure you are using a combination you like. If you are using a purchased product, be sure to follow the directions for application and safe handling.

Process for applying wax or oil

CLEAR COATS

Various clear coating products are available on the market. There are resins, polyurethanes, and lacquers, all of which work slightly differently and have varying results, but all provide a durable clear finish for metal. These products come in paint cans to be brushed on, or can be purchased as spray cans. Some cheaper clear coats tend to break down and peel in the sun, so I recommend buying something higher quality. These products often have the options of gloss, satin, and matte, which range from most shiny to least—you will have to decide which look you like best. These also will change the look of a patina or stain, unless specifically noted otherwise, so testing is recommended. Be sure to follow all safety instructions for the use and disposal of these products.

Close-up of a clear coated object, no patina or other color finish applied. A good clear coat should disappear once it has cured.

Projects

This section features a series of projects with step-by-step directions for you to follow. The projects start simple and get more complex—each new project building on the skills learned in the previous one. It is important to be excited and interested in what you are making, so whenever possible, I point out places where you can make changes so the piece you are working on is unique to your style and needs. If you have done some blacksmithing before, you may have encountered projects like these already. If you want to skip around, please go ahead, but you may wish to read through the directions and see if I offer any new and useful tips.

Remember, you are learning—either starting for the first time or somewhere at the beginning of your journey. Go easy on yourself; don't expect to be great at the very beginning. Don't compare yourself to anyone else but you. The point is your *own* progression and improvement, which will happen. When you look at the photographs I have included, remember that I have made each of these objects tens if not hundreds of times before. Plus, you never know how many examples I might have made to get the one that I liked best for the photo. If you are discouraged, remind yourself that the only way to get better is to keep practicing. Every blacksmith that you know of and whose work you admire had to start right here, at the very beginning. Don't compare your work to theirs, or to anyone else's. Keep your old projects so you remember where you started and can track your progress.

Before you start each project, you should read through the directions thoroughly, so you know where you are going, you can plan your materials, and you can set up your space with the tools you will need close by. It would also be beneficial to refer to the realignment exercise on page 31. Once your forge is hot and your body and mind are focused, get your hammer in your hand, heat up that metal, and start to swing!

TAPERS

The following three projects will introduce you to forging through the process of forming a taper—a common design element in blacksmithing that can be incorporated into almost any project. There are two main types of taper: pointed and flat. They are a simple form to hammer, add visual interest, and show that the object you have made was hand forged.

Taper Project 1:

Nail Hook

This simple hook is pointed at one end so that it can be hammered directly into wood. I would recommend predrilling a hole in the wood so you don't split it—this predrilled hole should be smaller than the largest diameter of the sharpened length of your hook. This hook will not work in drywall unless it goes through it and into wood behind it. I would recommend using this hook outdoors or in a garage.

Techniques involved: Tapering, bending

Goals: Gain an understanding of the proper heat that metal should be for effective forging; begin to develop hand-eye coordination and hammer control.

Material: Round or square bar stock can be used, diameters up to ⅜ inch (1 cm). I recommend starting with 5 inches (12.7 cm) of ¼-inch (0.6cm) square stock.

The first step is to form a pointed taper at one end of your material by hammering along the length of your material, hitting with harder force as you get toward the end. This taper has four sides and comes to a point at the nail end of your nail hook.

As we mentioned on page 32, you want your metal to be *hot* hot. Because you will be using thin material for this project, you can get away with working cooler metal, but use this as an opportunity to start to train your eye for what the metal looks like when it is fully up to heat. This will become more important as you use larger material and forge more complicated shapes.

1. Grab your metal out of the forge and hold it flat on the surface of your anvil. Start hammering about 2 inches (5 cm) from the end, beginning with light blows and getting heavier as you move toward the end. (1a, 1b)
2. Make sure to hammer to the very end of the metal; your hammer face will be partly on the metal and partly over the face of the anvil. (1c)

1a

1b

1c

2

3

4

3. Rotate your metal 180 degrees and repeat this process on the second face.

4. Rotate back and forth (or all the way around) until you have hammered your material to a point. (2)

   If you are using round material, you will be creating these faces as you forge. Remember to pay attention to the heat of your metal and put it back in the forge as soon as it is too cold to move effectively. Your goal is to use as few heats as possible, but at the beginning the going will be slow and you will have to reheat often, especially with small material like this, which cools quickly.

   Once you finish the point, put your metal back in the forge with the other end in the heat. On this side, you will make a flat taper. This kind of taper goes from thick to thin in one dimension and stays the same width in the other dimension (see page 32 for a more detailed description).

5. When the metal is hot, pull it out and hold it flat on the anvil face. Starting again about 2 inches (5 cm) from the end, hammer with increasing force to the end of the material.

6. Rotate 180 degrees and hammer lightly along the length of the metal just to move it back to the initial width of the material you started with. (3)

7. Continue to forge until you have an acceptable flat taper. Your material is now tapered on both sides. (4)

8. When you look at this taper from the top, it will be a uniform width, but from the side it will transition from thick to thin. The goal is to have a nice clean taper where you can't tell exactly where the transition starts. (5)

   As a variation, you can let your flat taper spread out in the top dimension. This is called a billed taper. If you like this look, just pay attention to keeping the edges of the flare flat with even lighter blows. Utilize the benefit of the large, flat surface of your anvil face by flipping your material so that each side of the taper is alternately hammered into the anvil to achieve clean lines. (6) Again refer to the "Moving the Metal" in How to Forge chapter (see pg 32) for a more detailed description.

Continue to hold your material by the pointed taper. If you have a lighter-weight hammer, use it for the following steps.

9. Set the metal over the horn of your anvil, with the wider face of the flat taper facing upward and the end of the taper just hanging over the edge of the horn. (7)

5

6

7

8

9

10

10. Lightly hit the end of the taper hanging off the horn so that it begins to curve down.

11. Continue these light hits as you slowly feed the metal forward, allowing it to bend down and around the horn. Feed as much material forward as you think necessary to form a functional and pleasing-looking hook. (8)

12. You can also flip the metal to hold it under the horn, with the hook coming up toward you. Bring the end up and around with light hammer blows, pulling slightly toward you. (9)

13. Continue to adjust the hook until you are happy with the shape. The curve can also be adjusted on the face of the anvil, with light blows on the curved end to close the hook smaller. This is one case where your metal does not have to be *hot* hot; it can be somewhat cool and still bend enough for small adjustments. (10)

Tip: *The horn of your anvil is tapered, so the outside edge of it is at an angle. Hold your material at an angle, with the hot end pointing slightly more toward the point of the horn. Sight your material along the edge of the horn so that it is at a right angle to that edge. Otherwise, the hook will bend in more of a spiral, curving toward the point of the horn.*

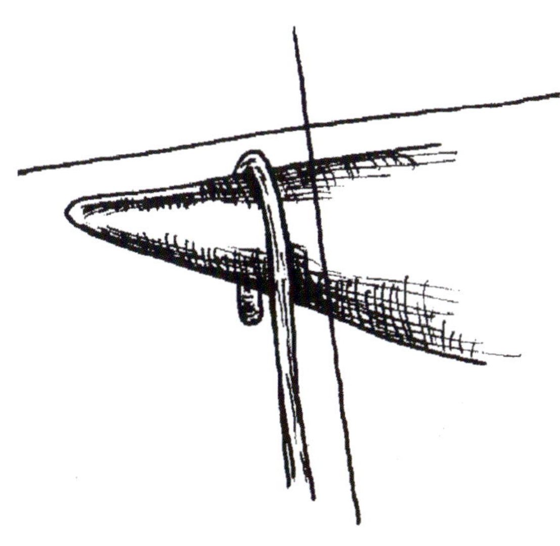

The last step is to bend your material into a right angle.

14. Reheat the pointed taper end of your metal. Hold it with your tongs on the curve or just below it where the curve ends. Bring it to the edge of the anvil, with the pointed taper hanging about 2 inches (5 cm) over the edge. Hammer that length down until it connects with the side of the anvil. (11a, 11b)

15. The face of your anvil is 90 degrees to its side, so you are using the corner of your anvil as a guide to copy that angle. You want the curve of your hook to be facing straight up and the straight part to be flat on the surface of the anvil. You may need to switch a few times between hammering the metal flat onto the face of the anvil and hammering the pointed end down until it contacts the side. You are not trying to squish the metal that you are hammering over the corner, as this will make it thinner. You also do not want a curved bend. Your goal is to get a crisp right angle.

16. Cool the metal in your quench bucket, and you are done. (12)

If you wish, you can use one of the finishing methods described on page 34.

Expansion options: Several types of finials—decorative shapes made on the ends of your metal—can be used on this hook to change up the design. You can also add other decorative elements such as twists (see page 60). Use the photo on the far right as an example, and get creative!

11a

11b

12

Taper Project 2:

S Hook

This project will help you practice most of the same techniques that were introduced with the nail hook (see page 40), but with a different result. An S hook is a common metal object that has many uses. At the end of these instructions, you will find suggestions for several variations; as always, you are encouraged to get creative.

Techniques involved: Tapering, bending

Goals: Gain an understanding of the proper heat that metal should be for effective forging; continue to develop hand-eye coordination and hammer control.

Material: Square material is easier for tapering, but I would recommend using something round for a different experience. Many sizes can be used, depending on your needs or taste. To differ from the nail hook (see page 40), use 6 inches (15 cm) of ⅜-inch (1cm) round stock.

Your first steps will be to taper both ends of your material. Now that you are familiar with tapers, you can choose which one you would like to use. Consider what you would like to practice, how you might use the hook once it is finished, and what you prefer aesthetically.

When you taper a piece of metal, you also lengthen it. Try measuring your material before and after each taper to see how much you are stretching it. Getting a feel for how much the metal moves is a helpful instinct to develop.

1. Heat and hammer each end to whatever taper you choose—they can be the same or different. (1)

   Remember, your goal is to use as few heats as possible.

2. Curve each side of your material over the horn of your anvil, using the same techniques as for the nail hook (see page 45). (2)

   Make sure that the ends curve in opposite directions. You can choose to curve both sides equally, so the hooks are the same size, or make one larger and one smaller.

3. That's it; you've made an S hook. (3)

1

2

3

4

5

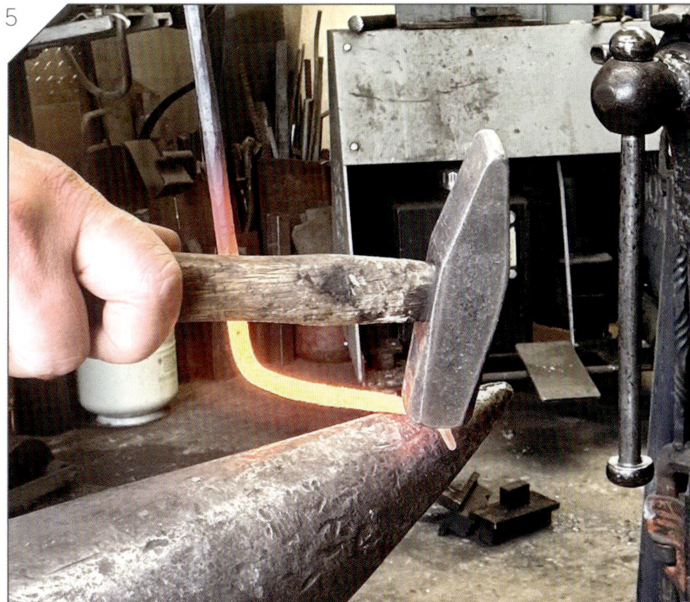

6

Expansion options: An alternative design that I like is something I call a "straight-backed S hook." You will use a longer piece of material for this, but the diameter can be whatever you like, as with the original version.

1. Follow Step 1 for the basic S hook (see page 50).
2. Bend each side down at a right angle, again in opposite directions. (4)
3. Curve the bent lengths of material on either end over your horn to make each hook. (5)
4. Be sure to hold your material so the middle length is pointing straight up from the horn. The right-angled bend will open somewhat, but you want to keep it mostly intact to achieve the circular look of the hook. (6)

You can add various finials and twists to either of these hooks, which you will learn in the next section.

Taper Project 3:

Spoon

Since it is made of mild steel, this spoon should not be used for regular eating. In the future, you could make it out of stainless steel, but that requires a bit more knowledge of material. It could be used as a salt or sugar spoon, as an espresso tamper, or for measuring out other dry goods. Think about your living situation and your daily life; what could you use a special spoon for to make a simple activity more delightful and satisfying?

Techniques involved: Spreading out, mid-material tapering, dishing, bending

Goals: Develop hammer control and accuracy, learn to spread out material into a consistent shape and thickness, make a simple tool, learn how to use a ball peen hammer to dish metal.

Material: Square or round material will work, but I would recommend round for this project, both for practice and because it will be easier to forge the scoop. The size of material you choose will determine the size of the scoop of the spoon, so you can't go too small. You don't want something super-large either, because you will need to draw it down to form the handle. I would not recommend using anything smaller than ⅜ inch (1 cm). In the accompanying photos, I am using 4 inches (10 cm) of ½-inch (1.3cm) round stock for a nice short scoop.

Before we begin, we need to define which part of the material will be the scoop and which will be the handle. There are several ways to do this, depending on the kinds of tools you have. This first step will describe how to do this with just a hammer and anvil.

1. Hold your material hanging over the far edge of your anvil at a downward-facing angle. (1)

   The section that hangs over the edge will be your scoop. It should be slightly longer than the diameter of your material if you want a round scoop, and longer if you want an oval-shaped scoop.

   Choose a section of your anvil edge that is not super sharp but not too rounded. In some anvils, the edge will be more rounded toward the horn and sharper toward the heel. If you don't have any variation in the edge of your anvil, just use what you've got.

2. Hammer the material into the edge of your anvil to make a divot, or neck, in the material. (2)

   Rotate your material slightly, keeping the edge of the anvil in line with the divot, and hammer again. Continue to do this until there is a divot all the way around your material

3. You can use the face of your hammer with the edge lined up with the edge of the anvil, or use the cross peen of your hammer. Either way, it is important to be as accurate as possible with your hammer blows so you create a clean neck. At the end of this step, you should have a piece of material with a neck that defines what will become the scoop and what will become the handle. (3)

Tip: *Be careful that you do not neck your material too much. You don't want your spoon to be weak and possibly break here during the rest of your forging. The thickness of the neck depends on the thickness of your starting material and your final design. In this example, the neck of this spoon is about ¼ inch (0.6 cm) in diameter.*

1

2

3

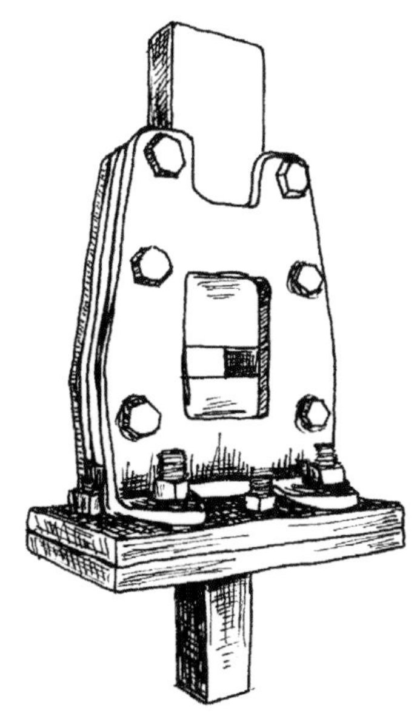

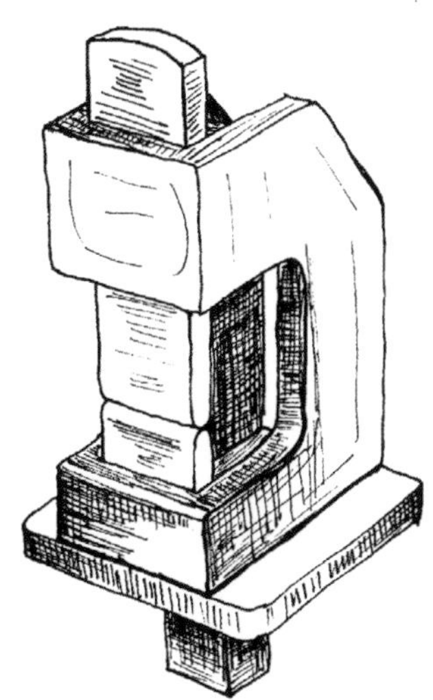

Examples of two possible guillotine tools

Alternative tools: The steps opposite require a steady hand and good hammer control, but the process can be made easier with different tools. You can purchase various tools or figure out how to make them yourself (see page 96), but these types of tools are a little more complicated than fits the scope of this book.

Basically, you need something with the same-shaped top and bottom that you can put your material in the middle of, then you hammer the top of the tool into the bottom of the tool, shaping your material equally on both sides. Two common types of tools that do this are spring swages and guillotine tools. You need just enough hammer control to hit the tool, and you can rotate your material to get a clean neck all the way around.

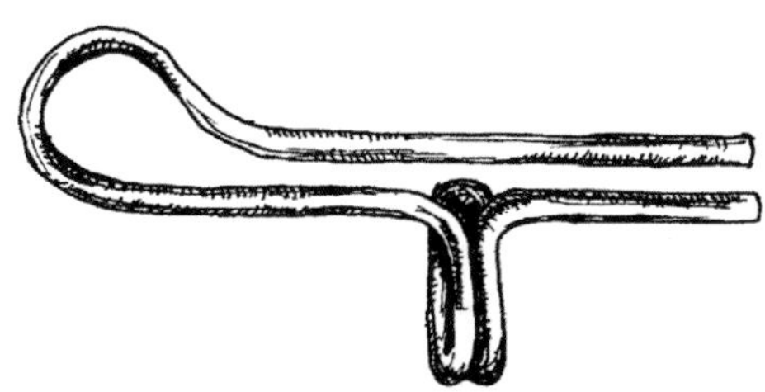

Spring swage

Your next stage is to taper and draw out the handle. We do this before flattening and shaping the scoop because that process will create a thin piece of metal that can be burned during repeated heats. Usually, you want to do the most delicate part of your forging last, so it will not be damaged while you shape the other areas. Determining the order of operations for a project is a useful skill to develop. This taper will be in the middle of your material instead of at the end. You want the handle to taper from thin at the neck you just made to wider at the end of the handle.

4. Hold your material by the piece that will become the scoop, with the scoop off the anvil and the handle section flat on the face of the anvil. (4)

5. Using the face of your hammer, forge the material into a taper by hitting harder near the scoop and lighter as you move toward the end of the handle. Rotate and repeat until you have your desired taper. (5)

6. In this example I have made a billed taper, but you can choose your own preference. (6)

Now you will be spreading out the scoop of the spoon. You can do this with a flat-faced hammer, the cross peen of a hammer, or a ball peen hammer. I used a ball peen for this example.

7. Hold the metal by the handle. Place the material that will become the scoop on the horn, and hammer down into it. (7)

   Your goal is to spread the material wider, not longer. Think about applying your hammer blows to taper the material out to the sides instead of tapering along the length. Pay careful attention to how your metal moves with each hit, and adjust your hit target area to spread the metal into a round shape.

   The reason you hammer your material on the horn of the anvil instead of the face is to focus the force of your blow from both sides. The horn is slightly rounded, so it touches less surface area of your material. This means the metal will move more with each hit. It's the same idea as using a ball peen hammer instead of one with a flat face, just from the other side.

   To illustrate this concept, imagine holding a lump of clay in the flat of your hand. If you press with one finger in the middle of the clay, it will move evenly out from your finger. Placing your material on the horn of the anvil and hitting it with a ball or cross peen allows this principle to work from both sides.

4

5

6

7

8a

8b

If you use a cross peen, position it along the length of the material to pull it out wider on both sides. If you hit with the face of your hammer without intention, the material will just get longer, as with a taper.

If you don't have a cross peen or ball peen, you can still use the face of your hammer. Just adjust the angle at which you hit to use an edge of the face, or the heel of the hammer, instead of hitting it flat. Again, you are simply focusing the energy of your hammer blow into a smaller surface area to get the metal to move where you want.

Tip: *To get a nice round scoop, pay special attention to the back "corners" of the material on either side of the neck. Hit here to make sure your scoop is wide enough where it transitions from the handle (see the illustration below).*

8. Alternate between spreading the material on the horn and flattening it on the face of your anvil with the face of your hammer. Keep doing this until you have a consistently thin, round shape on the end of your handle. (8a, 8b)

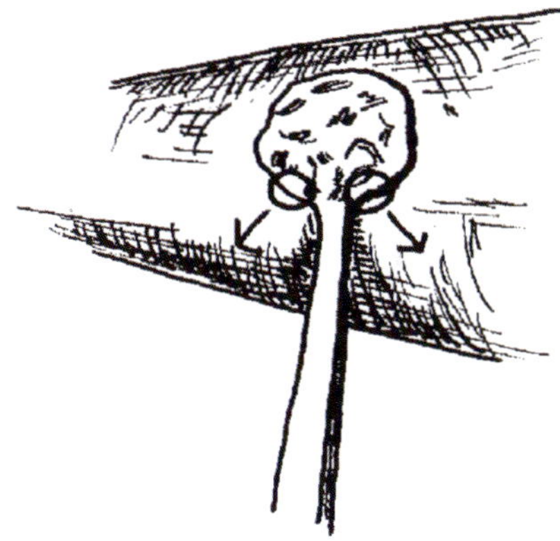

9. If , like mine, your shape is not perfectly clean, use tools to shape it. You can use an angle grinder, a belt sander, or a file.

The next step is to cup the scoop. You can do this without any other tool by just using the hardy hole, but this will be difficult and not very clean. The following instructions show you how to make your first simple tool.

MAKING A HOLLOW TOOL TO FORM THE SCOOP

We need something that is round but hollow in the middle, so you can hammer your scoop into it to form the cup. There are tools specifically for this purpose: either smaller swage tools or a larger swage block. But if you don't have those, this tool works very well.

Material: The size of material you use depends on the size of your scoop. For this example, I used ½-inch (1.3cm) round material, starting with about 6 inches (15 cm).

10. Hold your material over the edge of your horn and hammer it down so it curves all the way around and past itself. (9)

11. Adjust the circle on the face of your anvil until the outside diameter is just a little smaller than the diameter of your scoop. (10)

    If the circle gets too small, you can open it by placing it around the horn and hammering it on the curve of the circle. You can also shrink it by hammering it on the face.

12. When the circle is cool, cut it where the two legs overlap. (11)

    You can use an angle grinder, a bandsaw, or a hacksaw to do this. If you don't have any of these tools, you can start with the exact length of material you need to make the circle to the correct diameter, but it is difficult to make a perfect circle in this way.

13. Heat your circle and hammer the two ends flat. You want the ends to meet up as cleanly as possible to avoid making a mark on the bottom of your scoop. (12)

14. If you are having trouble getting the ends to line up correctly, it may help to clamp the circle in a vice, with the seam facing up, and hammer one side of the seam or the other into line. (13)

    If you really do not want to make a circle this way, just slice off a section of pipe that is the correct diameter. However, because the pipe has sharper edges the bottom of your spoon will not be smooth. You also need a pipe with at least 1/8-inch (3mm) thick walls, or it will collapse under your hammer.

FINISHING THE SPOON

15. Place the cooled circle on the face of your anvil and heat up the scoop of your spoon.

16. Hammer the scoop down into the middle of the circle. Rotate and change the angle of the spoon as needed to get a nice shape. (14)

9

10

11

12

15

13

16

14

17. If you don't have a ball peen hammer, use the corner or edge of the face of your hammer.

18. Finish your handle however you like. For this example, I made a simple curve by hammering the handle down over the horn, which you have practiced several times now. (15)

Expansion options: There are many ways you can customize this design, from using different sizes of material to adding twists and other decorative elements to the handle. In the photo above, I used 3 inches (7.5 cm) of ¾-inch (2cm) material. Since this is rather large, I used my power hammer to forge down the handle, but it is certainly possible to do this by hand. (16)

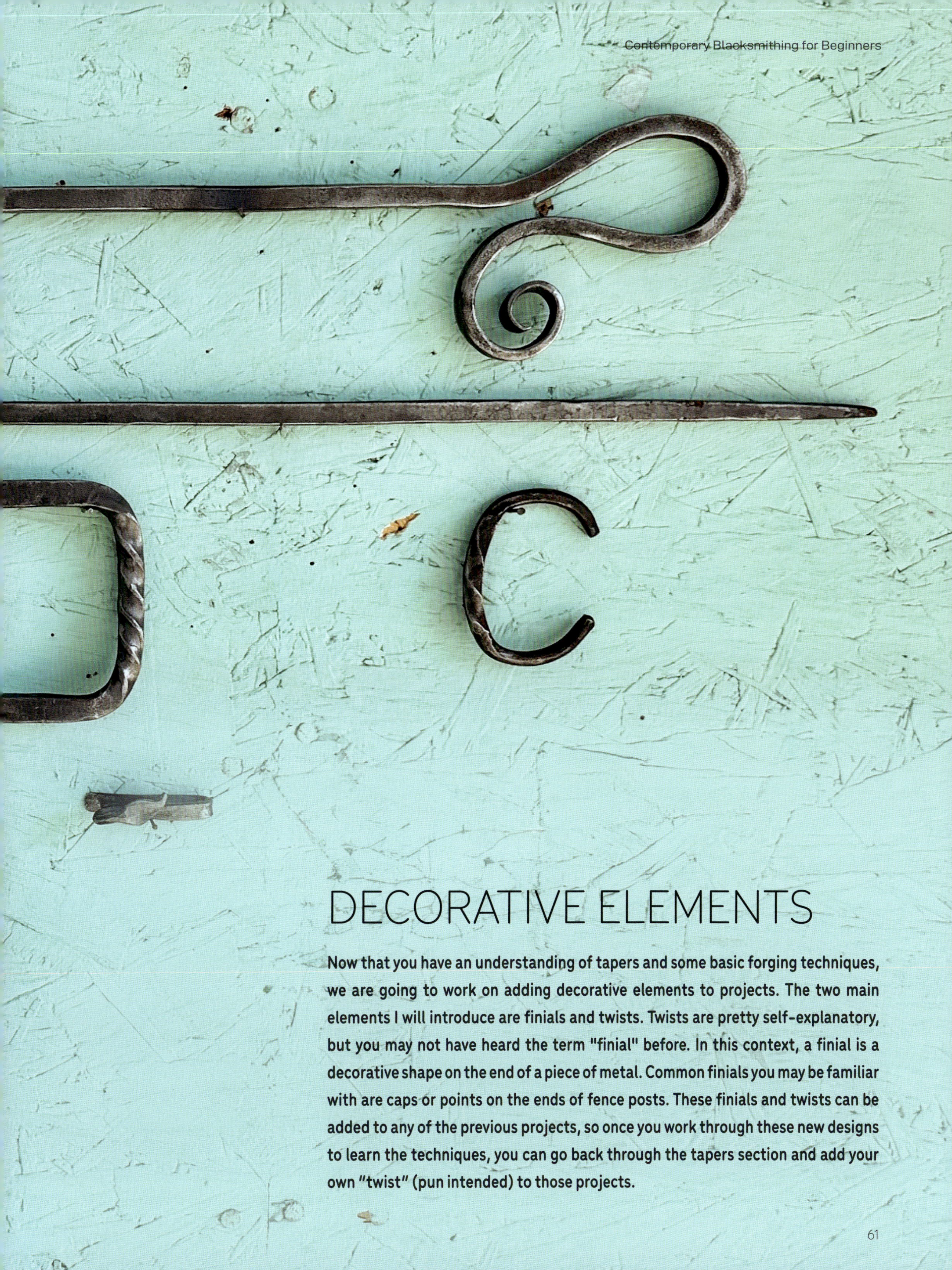

DECORATIVE ELEMENTS

Now that you have an understanding of tapers and some basic forging techniques, we are going to work on adding decorative elements to projects. The two main elements I will introduce are finials and twists. Twists are pretty self-explanatory, but you may not have heard the term "finial" before. In this context, a finial is a decorative shape on the end of a piece of metal. Common finials you may be familiar with are caps or points on the ends of fence posts. These finials and twists can be added to any of the previous projects, so once you work through these new designs to learn the techniques, you can go back through the tapers section and add your own "twist" (pun intended) to those projects.

Decorative Elements Project 1:

Leaf Finial Key Hook

This key hook will introduce you to your first finial, a simple leaf. I initially designed this object because I am a disliker of belts and a liker of not having a wad of keys in my pocket. This simple hook enables me to hang my keys on my pants without a belt. Problem solved! If you are an enjoyer of belts, this project can easily be adapted to fit over one.

Techniques involved: Spreading metal wider, forging a middle taper, fitting to a specific use, adjusting metal cold

Goals: Develop hammer control and accuracy; develop finesse and speed by working small.

Material: While you could use larger material to get a larger leaf, you don't want a huge chunk of metal hanging off your pants, so I strongly recommend using ¼-inch (0.6 cm) diameter. You could use square, but I find round to result in a nicer-looking leaf. For this demonstration, I am using 4 inches (10 cm) of ¼-inch (0.6cm) round stock.

1. Forge a short, pointed taper on the very end of your material. (1)

   It will be helpful to angle your material and your hammer dramatically in order to get as short a taper as possible. With this small amount of material, you can always use a smaller hammer than usual to create this point. If you end up with a long taper, you will have a long leaf, which is fine—it just depends on what you think looks best. I like a short, round leaf, so that is what I am planning for at this stage.

2. Place the point on the horn of the anvil and hammer to pull out the "cheeks" of the leaf. (2)

   This is similar to the spoon, but in this case you do not want to spread out the point of your taper, since that will be the point of the leaf. You can use a ball peen hammer or any hammer with a smaller face. This is a smaller material, and you need to be precise with your hits, so use whatever hammer you can control well.

   Think about the leaf with a line down the middle. You are taking material from each side and pinching/pulling it out. Your blows should only hit the half of the material that you are working on. With the side of the leaf facing toward the rest of the anvil, your blows should scoop slightly toward you. When working the other side of the leaf, your blows should push away. It will probably feel easier to work the side that is closest to you, so you can always flip the leaf over to forge each side in the same position. (3)

1

2

3

4a

4b

3. Once you have your desired width of the leaf, you need to finish the point. If you want the leaf to be a bit longer, you can draw the point out. I like to use the horn of my anvil to forge a slight curl in the end of my leaf. (4a, 4b)

The next step is to create a taper in the middle of your material, using the same techniques as the spoon (see page 56). This will become the stem of the leaf.

4. Hang the leaf off the edge of the anvil and start forging at the transition from the leaf to the stem. (5)

   The smallest part of the taper starts at the neck of the leaf and gets larger toward the other end of the material. You can start this taper while holding the end of the material opposite the leaf, but you will have to flip it to hold from the leaf to finish the taper.

   Flip your material so you hold it by the leaf with the rest of the length in the forge.

5. Continue drawing out the taper and end with a flat taper. Make sure the flat is in the same plane as the leaf. (6)

   This also stretches your material, which is needed for the hook to work, so make sure you get to at least 5 inches (12.7 cm) long (not counting the leaf). I like to maintain some of the roundness of the stem of the leaf, so I don't forge the taper all the way back. I think it looks nice when the rounded stem blends into the flattened taper.

5

6

6. Holding the tapered end, hang the stem and leaf over your horn and hammer to bend it down and around. (7)

   This bend is where your key ring will hang, so it needs to be large enough to easily slip the ring over the leaf, but not so large that the keys could fall off. (8)

7. Holding your material by the bend you just made, hang 2 inches (5 cm) at least (err on the side of a little more) off the face of the anvil and bend it down at 90 degrees. (9)

7

8

9

10

12b

11

12a

8. Flip your material so the leg of the bend is upright on your anvil. Hammer it toward yourself and down so it is almost touching itself. You should be able to do this in the same heat as the previous step. (10)

   This bend is where the hook will fit over the waistband or pocket of your pants, so you don't want it all the way closed, just enough to fit snugly. The size of the bend can be adjusted cold, so just get something that seems close for now.

9. Adjust both of the bends so the hook fits both your pants and your keys. (11)

10. Cool the material and test how it fits. You could hook it over the waistband of your pants, on one of the pockets, or however else will work for you! Try it out, see where you like it, and adjust as needed. (12a, 12 b)

Expansion options: This design can easily be changed to make different objects. For example, you could forge the leaf and then forge the rest of the material into a simple circle to be used as a keychain ornament, or—with a smaller circle—a necklace pendant. You could also start with a longer piece of material and bend the extra length back toward itself in an oblong loop for a belt to go through. Now that you know how to forge a leaf, you can add it as a decorative element to any other project.

Decorative Elements Project 2:

Scrolled Shepherds' Hooks

A shepherd's hook is a common decorative element for yards or gardens. It is often used to hang a potted plant, bird feeder, or outdoor lantern; however, there are plenty of imaginative uses for something with a similar design. For example, it is easily adapted into a simple fire poker. I will be detailing both options in the instructions. For the fire poker, I will be making what I call a recurve scroll, so you have something different to try. Think about your living situation, or perhaps a good friend or family member. Is there a version of this that might fit well into your lives?

Techniques involved: Scrolling, working with longer material

Goals: Learn how to make an even scroll.

Material: A shepherd's hook can be tall, but since this version will not have a support leg (we will be making a more complex option that does later) you don't want it to be too heavy. The same goes for a fire poker—length is good, but if it's too heavy it's not very useful. As always, use your own discretion for what material will work best for your intended use. In the examples, I am using 32 inches (81 cm) of ⅜-inch (1cm) square material for both objects.

Both options for this project have a flat taper at one end and a pointed taper at the other. We will start by forging the more complex parts of the project and finish with the simple pointed taper.

Forge a flat or billed taper (your choice) in one end of your material. The length of the taper is up to you, but I recommend making it a little long so you have more material to work with. Material for both my hook and the poker were tapered to 34 inches (86 cm).

For the shepherd's hook, I made one large scroll; the handle for the fire poker is what I call a recurved scroll. The large scroll is easiest, so we'll start with that.

SIMPLE SCROLL

Forming the scroll starts in a similar way to making a hook; you just keep hammering the metal around the horn so it curls up on itself.

It is important to get this first curve looking nice, because it is hard to come back and correct it once you've made the rest of the scroll. You don't want to have a flat end, but you also don't want to curve it so much that it touches itself.

1. Hang the end of your taper over the horn and hammer it down. Feed your metal forward as you hammer until you have a small hook. (1)
2. Place your metal flat on the face of your anvil, with the curved end up, and tap it toward you to continue the scroll. You can lift the end of the material up or drop it down to adjust the angle of your hits. Continually flip the curve flat so you can look at it, and don't hammer too far. (2a, 2b)

1

2a

2b

3. Continue curving the material by using the horn again, hammering toward you on the face of the anvil, or whatever other method you devise until you are happy with how it looks. (3)

   Again, constantly check the curve from the side so you can see how it is developing, and hammer the scroll flat if it gets wonky. If you have a billed taper, make sure you adjust so you don't have one flat side.

   A nice-looking scroll is one where the space between the spirals widens at a consistent ratio. Think about the outside of a snail shell or the curve of a young fern leaf. Nature is beautiful naturally.

   Functionality is also important. To decide when my scroll was finished, I thought about how the object would be used. I wanted to be able to hang something with a large diameter, so I made sure the inside of the scroll, from which an object would hang, was about 4½ inches (11.5 cm) from the vertical leg. This means I can hang something as large as 9 inches (23 cm) in diameter.

3

RECURVE SCROLL

If you want to try a recurve scroll, there are several more steps. Start the same way but stop with just a small scroll.

1. Heat the whole scroll and several inches of flat material. Take your hot metal out of the forge and dip the scrolled end in your quench bucket to cool it to dark metal.

   Do this as quickly as possible so you retain heat where you want it. Wherever the metal is cool, it will not move; where it is hot, it will.

2. Place the scroll facing up over the edge of your horn and hammer it down and around. (4)

   Your scroll should be cool enough that it will not change shape. Adjust until you like it.

   I am suggesting that this option is to be used for a fire poker; in which case, the scroll will be the handle, so it is important for it to feel right in your hand. Angling the scroll off the body of the material will help with both the feel and functionality.

3. Place the second bend over the horn of the anvil and hammer it down while slightly lifting the end of the material you are holding up. (5)

4

5

6

7

8

4. Adjust the curve on the face of the anvil or the horn (or both) until you decide it is done. (6)

5. Whatever scroll you are making, forge a pointed taper on the other end of your material. (7)

   The length is up to you, but a slightly longer taper will mean your shepherd's hook can go farther into the ground. Don't make your fire poker too long or it will be too off-balance to use comfortably.

6. Heat the unforged middle of your material and hammer it on the diamond to "break" the manufactured corners. (8)

   You could do this after you have finished your scroll and before the pointed taper, or even as the first step before you forge any tapers. If you are working on a long piece, this will take several heats. The goal is for the whole piece to be heated and hammered so it has a uniform look and texture. These details add a lot to your work.

7. If you are making the fire poker, add a right-angle bend to the end to help you move logs around in the fire. (9)

Expansion options: Both projects would be great to add twists to, which you will learn next. You don't have to do anything different; you can use the same objects you just finished and simply reheat them to add a twist. A version with a leaf finial would be quite nice for the shepherd's hook, which will feature in the garden.

Decorative Elements Project 3:

Simple Twist Bracelet or Handle

Twists are a fairly simple way to add visual and tactile interest to your work. There are many types of twists—you may even come up with your own variations. We are starting with a very simple twist, then flattening it, which achieves a different look. The following instructions detail how to make a twist using a vice; however, if you don't have a vice, there are still ways you can make this work. You'll just have to innovate, which is one of the aspects of blacksmithing that I love.

Techniques involved: Using a twisting fork and vice, drawing material down to forge it from thicker to thin, forging from square to round

Goals: Learn how to twist metal evenly, keep it straight, and straighten if necessary.

Material: Your material must have edges for the twist to show, and to securely grab both ends to actually make the twist, so you need to use square or flat material instead of round. The size of the material depends on what you want to make. The first project option here is a bracelet, but I am also providing instructions to forge a handle or drawer pull. Here, I am using 4 inches (10 cm) of a 3/8 -inch (1cm) square for the bracelet and 10 inches of 1/2 square for the handle.

1. Mark the section of your material that you will be twisting. For the bracelet, this was a 2-inch (5cm) section in the middle. (1)

   Tip: *You will need to mark your material with something you can see when it is hot (a pencil or marker will just burn off). Welders' soapstone or a silverstreak pencil will not burn off but can be very difficult to see. The best option is to mark with a chisel or punch, if you have one.*

2. Clamp one end of your material in the vice, lining up your mark with the outside edge of the vice. Grab the other end at the mark with a twisting fork and twist the number of times you desire. (2)

   Twisting forks can be made or bought, or you can use a crescent wrench. If you don't have a vice, can you clamp one end to a worktable or your anvil? Do you have someone who can help you by holding that end with another wrench? Look at what you have available, and get creative.

   One twist means one face rotates 90 degrees. For the bracelet, I twisted three times. Keep in mind that you can twist only while your metal is hot, so you need to be quick. You also want to keep your twists even. Where the metal is cooler, it will be a looser twist; where it is hotter, it will be tighter.

   Because your vice will be drawing heat out of your material, the side in the vice will cool faster. If you don't get enough twists in the first heat, you can heat it up and twist some more, but you will have to be thoughtful about where the heat is and try not to tighten the twists you already have.

If you like the look of this twist as it is, you can skip the next step of flattening. However, flattening results in a more interesting twist and makes the bracelet sit nicely on a wrist.

3. Place the twist on the face of your anvil and hammer flat. (3)
4. Place your piece so one untwisted section is on the face of the anvil and the rest is hanging off the edge toward you.
5. Hammer that untwisted section down, rotating to hammer each face until your material is about ¼ inch (0.6 cm) in diameter. (4)

   This is similar to the tapering process, but you are keeping the metal square and the same width while lengthening it. This is called drawing the material down. It is also a practice of hammer control, since you are trying to keep the transition from twist to smaller material clean and not hammer the twist. Remember to relax your body, hold the material still and flat on the anvil, stand up straight, and engage your core.

6. Adjust the angle of your material so you are now holding it over the face of the anvil on the diamond, with one corner of the square up and one resting on the anvil. (5)
7. Hammer down the corners to make an octagon. Continue hammering and rotating your material until the square is round. (6)

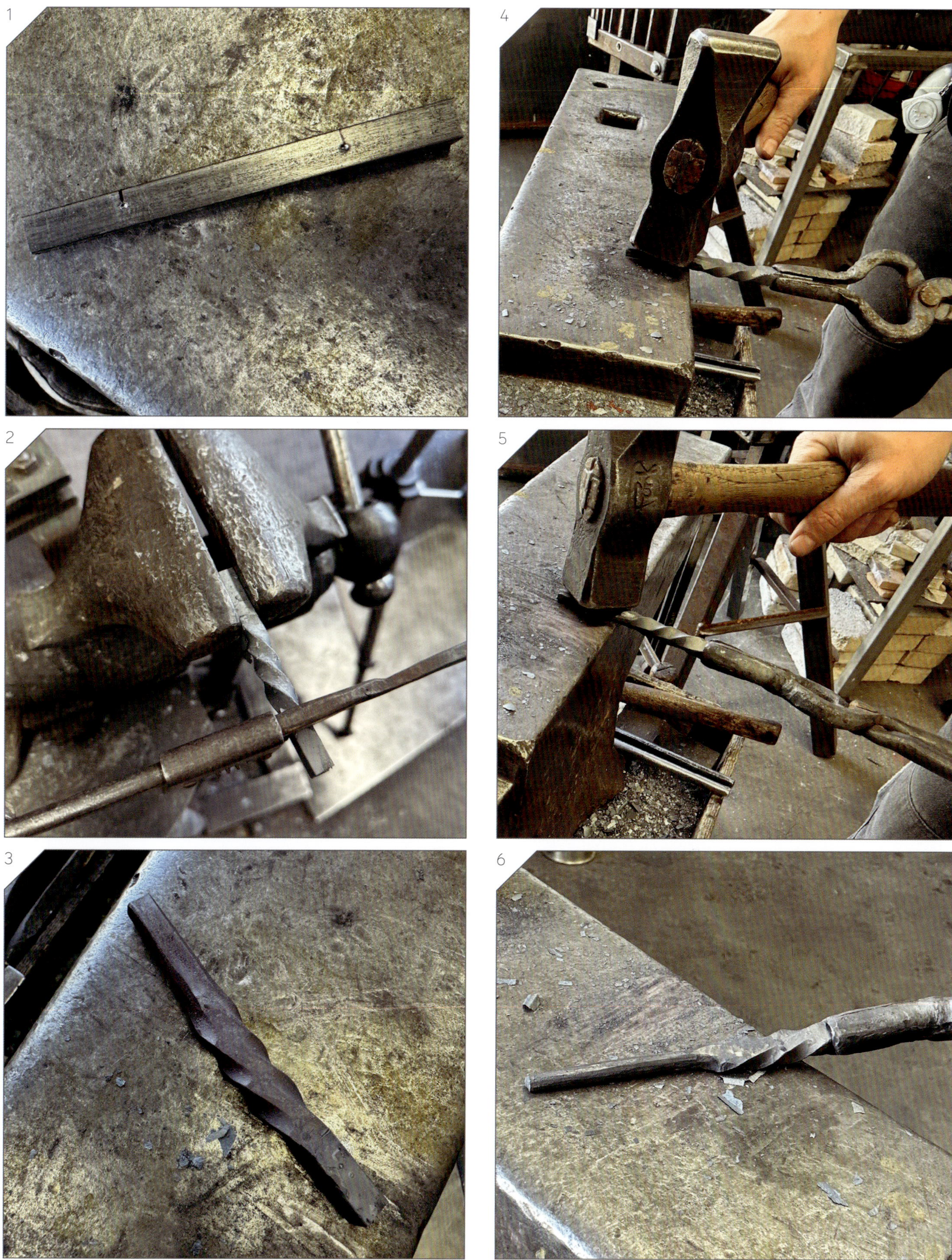

8. Repeat Steps 6–7 on the other leg of your material. (7)

Your material may have gotten a bit bent and out of alignment during this process. There is a way to flatten it without messing up your twist.

9. Place a piece of wood on your anvil. A 2 x 4 works nicely, but something thinner will do as well.
10. Using a wooden or rawhide mallet, hammer your piece flat. The wood will burn a bit, but that's okay. Just protect yourself from the smoke with a respirator if necessary. (8)
11. Bend both rounded ends of your material over the horn to create an oval shape. Keep a gap wide enough to slip over your wrist from the side. (9a, 9b)

    The gap in my bracelet is about 1¼ inches in the middle of the material; if it is much smaller, you may need to cut the ends shorter. Whatever you do, don't try anything on until you have cooled your metal!
12. Adjust the shape of your bracelet (hot or cold) until it fits as you want it.

    Since this is a worn object that touches the skin, I recommend finishing it with something nontoxic, like coconut oil or plain beeswax. (10)

HANDLE OPTION

If you're not into the idea of a bracelet, this is a similar object you can make. You can use larger material; here I used ½-inch (1.3cm) square. Mark the twist area at 3¼ inches (8.3 cm) in the middle of the material, and follow the instructions until Step 4 (or Step 3 if you don't want a flattened twist). I twisted three times instead of six, as I think it looks better.

1. Straighten your twist on wood, if needed.
2. Hold your material so about 1 inch (2.5 cm) hangs off the smallest point of the horn.
3. Hammer that piece of material down into a right angle.
4. Repeat this step on the other end.
5. If you have a post vice, these bends can be made even easier by clamping each leg in the vice and bending the twist with your tongs.
6. Flatten your material, if needed, making sure that both bent ends are in the same plane. (11)

To make this pull or handle usable, you will have to drill a hole vertically into the face of each bent end and cut threads in it, called tapping. This requires tools and knowledge that you may or may not have, and is beyond the scope of this book—if it is something you want to do, figure out how to learn it! (12)

> **Expansion options:** The next project teaches a reverse twist (see page 89). This could be used for a bracelet as well. There are also other twists you can learn later, such as a pineapple twist, which requires the use of a chisel—a tool that you will be making later (see page 98).

The handle piece in the photographs is sized for cupboards or drawers, but it could be scaled up by using larger material for a door handle. It could be made using other twists as well.

7

8

9a

11

9b

12

10

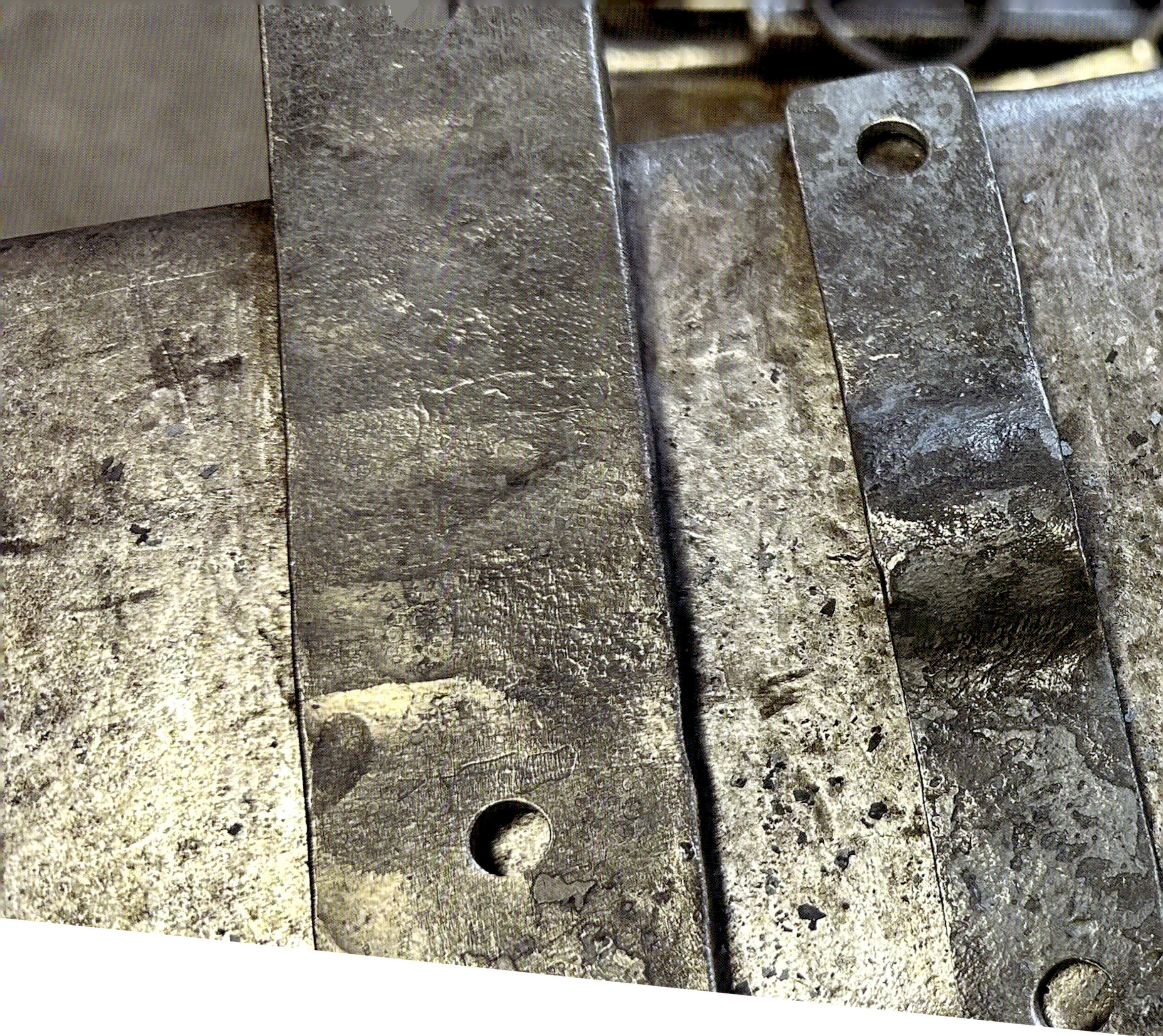

Decorative Elements Project 4:

Reverse Twist Door Knocker

This project introduces you to the reverse twist, which is more complicated than the twist used in the previous project. It also uses multiple pieces of metal and requires drilling holes. There is an option to use fewer pieces that I will point out. If you do not have a way to drill holes, you can simply wait to complete this project until you have made your rounded punch, which is coming up in the next section.

Techniques involved: Keeping track of amount and direction of twist, rounded taper, fitting multiple pieces together

Goals: Forge an even reverse twist, keep twist corners sharp, and forge a clean circle.

Material: There are several pieces of varying sizes and shapes in this project; you can adjust as needed and according to what you have available. The following measurements were used for the example in the photographs:

Knocker: 8 inches (20 cm) of ⅝-inch (1.6cm) square
Bent holder: 5 inches (12.7 cm) of ¼ × 1 inch (0.6 × 2.5 cm) flat bar
Backing plate: 9 inches (23 cm) of ¼ × 1¾ inch (0.6 × 4.5 cm) flat bar

Since there are multiple pieces, I will break down the steps for each piece, starting with the easiest.

BACKING PLATE

This one is really simple. All you need to do is throw this in the forge to heat up so some scale is created and it looks consistent with the other pieces. You can hammer it a bit for texture if you want.

If you want to simplify this project, you don't totally need this piece, but your door will get dented without it. You will drill or punch holes in this piece at a later step (see page 88).

BENT HOLDER

1. Taper each end of this piece in a flat taper. (1)

   My finished piece was 6 inches (15 cm) long. You could bill it out if you want, make it longer so the knocker hits it and doesn't need a backing plate, or any other changes you can think of.

2. Using the horn, forge a slight bend in the middle of the piece (not a full bend around). (2)

   You want the bend to be right in the middle of the piece, so you can mark it first or just eyeball and adjust.

The next step is to bend the legs back without removing the middle bend.

3. Hold one leg of the piece in your tongs, with the bend facing down.

4. Place the bend at the edge of the anvil, just a little lower than the face, so 2½ inches (6.4 cm) of the leg is over the face of the anvil. Hammer the leg down until it touches the face. (3)

1

2

3

4

5a

5b

5. Repeat Steps 3–4 on the other side of the piece. (4)

   You may need to re-bend the middle over the horn again as you adjust the legs, especially if your first leg was too bent.

6. Place the piece on the face of the anvil, with the middle bend facing up. Hammer each leg down to make sure they are in the same plane. (5a, 5b)

   Don't hammer the middle bend down; you need enough space for the knocker to rotate. You can even place a piece of scrap material under the bend to make sure it stays at the right height.

This next section involves using a drill to make the mounting holes in the piece you just made. If you do not have a drill, you can create these holes with the round punch tool you will be making later. These steps should be made only after the metal is cool.

7. Mark the middle of each leg at ½ inch (1.3 cm) from the end. (7)

   I like to use a fine-point Sharpie to be as accurate as possible.

8. Line a center punch up on the marks and hit a clean blow with your hammer. (8)

   This puts a divot in the metal to keep your drill on track or guide your use of a round punch.

9. Drill these holes or heat your material back up and punch them. (9)

   If drilling, the size of the holes should be based on what kind of screw you will be using to attach the knocker.

7

8

9

10

11

12

KNOCKER

1. Mark your material with a 1-inch (2.5cm) section in the middle. (10)

   As with the simple twist (see page 76), you will need to mark this with something that can be seen when the metal is hot. The middle 1 inch (2.5 cm) will be the flat part of the twist, and 2 inches (5 cm) on either side will be twisted.

Next is tapering each end. This will be similar to a pointed taper, but it will not come all the way to a point; it should stop at about ⅜-inch (1cm) square. You could do the twist first, but I wanted the look of the twist itself being tapered. Since this is fairly thick material, I will outline a different method of tapering that is more aggressive and will help you move the material faster.

2. Place the material on the horn of your anvil. Starting from the middle inch mark farthest from you and moving to the end, hammer into the horn while pulling your piece toward you. Increase the strength of your blows as you get to the end of the material. (11)

3. Rotate and forge each face the same way.

   Your result will be lumpier than hammering on the face of the anvil, so periodically clean it up by returning to the face. This method moves the metal more dramatically because you are reducing the surface area touching the bottom of the material, increasing the force of each blow and essentially forging from both sides at once.

4. Forge the taper on the other leg. The total length of your piece should be around 12 inches (30.5 cm). (12)

Next you will be marking your material and making the actual twist. Again, if you do not have a vice, you will have to be creative.

5. Using a method that will be visible on hot metal, mark 2 inches (5 cm) on either side of the 1-inch (2.5cm) middle mark. (13)
6. Clamp one leg in the vice, on the farthest side of the 2-inch (5cm) mark.
7. Place your twisting fork on the outside of the 1-inch (2.5cm) middle mark that is closest to the vice, so 2 inches (5 cm) of material is being twisted. (14)
8. Twist. (15)

   I did three twists on my piece, but you can choose the number you want, keeping in mind the same factors about heat that were outlined in the previous project. Make sure to keep track of the direction you are twisting. I twisted to the right, clockwise.

13

14

15

16

17

18

Next is the second twist, which needs to be in the opposite direction to the first. This can be a bit of a mind game, so go slowly and think through each action.

9. Clamp the other leg in the vice, paying the same attention to the marks. Place the twisting fork at the 1-inch (2.5cm) mark and twist the same number of times but in the opposite direction. (16)
10. Flatten your piece, using the wood method from the previous project. (17)

    Your next step is to round out the tapers you made on each end. Do not do this step before twisting, because it is difficult to hold round material in a vice. You can choose how much or little you want the material to be rounded. For functionality, it is important to have at least ½ inch (1.3 cm) of the end rounded so it rotates in the holder smoothly. I forged the round back a bit more but left some transition back to square before the twist.

11. Hold your taper on the face of the anvil, with one corner of the squared material facing up and one on the face of the anvil (on the diamond).
12. Hammer each corner flat, making sure not to hammer the twist.
13. Continuously rotate your piece as you hammer to bring it completely into round.
14. Repeat these steps on the other leg. (18)

The last stage is to bend this into a circle, without marring your twist.

15. Holding the twist just off the horn, hammer each leg down and around in a nice curve. (19)

16. Curve the other leg and adjust as needed. (20)

17. If you need to bend the twists themselves, place the middle flat of the twist at the tip of the horn, making sure no part of the twist is touching the horn.

18. Using a wooden or rawhide mallet, hammer the twist down to give it a curve.

19. Continue to adjust until you have a satisfactory circle.

The final stage will be to drill (or punch) holes in the backing plate.

20. Use the holes already in the holder piece and transfer them to the backing plate so they line up.

21. Drill the holes, or wait until you have made your round punch tool (see page 108) and punch them. (21)

19

20

21

22

24

23

22. Clean up and finish each piece separately. (22)

The screws shown are lag screws, and I have forged the heads from octagon to square. You can certainly use regular hex heads from any hardware store. I would recommend darkening them with a patina if they are shiny, so they look better with the forged metal. (23)

You can find square head lags online or in some stores, or, if you are careful, you can forge the heads yourself. Be cautious about safety and ventilation if you forge anything with a zinc coating, since zinc is toxic when it burns.

Expansion options: These directions are for a single reverse twist; it is also possible to make multiple reverse twists in a single piece, which looks quite dramatic. Use the same concepts outlined here, but once you do the first twist, you will have to cool that twist to make the second, then cool both to make the third, and so on.

In the photo above, I have used 12 inches (30.5 cm) of ½ inch (1.3 cm) square and made four twists. I also rounded the square ends so the knocker will rotate easily. (24)

Decorative Elements Project 5:

Ball End Finial: Choose Your Own Adventure

This project will be a little different because I will not be giving you directions on what object to make. The steps will outline how to forge a ball on the end of a piece of material, and it will be up to you to decide which of the previous projects to add it to (the freestanding double hooks project specifically uses this technique on page 144, so you could also wait until then to try it out). The purpose of this book is to teach you how to be a blacksmith, not just how to follow directions to make the exact same object as me, and the point of this project is to give your mind some creativity to practice and some problems of your own to solve. Thinking creatively and coming up with an idea of something to make totally on your own is difficult. It's a mental muscle that you have to build up in the same way that you are building up your physical muscles to swing a hammer.

Techniques involved: Forging a ball on the end of a piece of material

Goals: Hammer control, precision

Material: Round material will be easier for this, but you can use square if you prefer. You can use various diameters of material, but ½ inch (1.3 cm) will likely be easiest—large enough to give you enough mass to make the ball, but not so large that it will be difficult to forge out the rest of the piece. The smaller material you use, the harder the process will be. For the photos, I made an S hook with a ball end, using 7½ inches (19 cm) of ½-inch (1.3cm) round.material

Your first step is to define the amount of material that you will be using to make this finial—a similar process to forging the spoon (see page 56). A ball, obviously, is the same diameter from top to bottom as it is from side to side. So, whatever size of material you are using, the length you use for the ball should be the same as the diameter of the material, with just a little extra to make up for some of the compression that will occur.

1. Hang the correct length of material over the far edge of your anvil at a downward angle. (1)
2. Hammer the material that is over the face of the anvil down into the edge so the underside is indented. (2)
3. Rotate your material 90 degrees to forge an indentation in the next "side."
4. Continue rotating until you have a clean neck in your material. Be sure to forge on the diamond as well if you are using square material. (3)

   You do not want to make your neck too thin, so control the strength of your blows.

1

2

3

4

5

6

5. Tip: Your hammer control needs to be as precise as possible when making this neck, so you do not deform the material you just defined. (4)

Tip: *You may find it more comfortable to use the near side of your anvil, with the ball end angled up.*

6. Rest the neck of your material on the edge of your anvil closest to you, with the ball end angled up.

   Choose a medium radius edge, if possible.

7. Hammer the edge of the face of your material down, rotating it as you hit. (5)

   With this step you will be shaping the edge of the ball that you are hitting, as well as the bottom of the ball that is against the anvil. Your blows should be moderated and even, to make a round instead of a squished shape. Be sure to hold your material with a little pressure so it stays tight to the anvil.

8. Holding your material in the same position, drop your tong hand even more and hit on the very end of the material, working it down into the ball. Continue to rotate the piece as you hammer, until the end of the ball is rounded. (6)

9. Angle the material so the top of the ball is resting on the face of the anvil.

10. Forge down the bottom surface of the ball where it meets the stem. (7)

11. Continue to hold at various angles and hammer as needed to refine the ball until you are satisfied with how it looks.

12. The rest of the project is up to you! Depending on what project you choose, you may just slightly taper the stem as it comes off the ball, or dimension all the material into a smaller diameter. (8)

Tip: *Whatever you choose, think through the order of operations to figure out when to add the ball.*

7

8

TOOLS

One of the great advantages of being a blacksmith is the ability to make your own tools. Not only does this teach you a lot about forging and metallurgy, but you can also invent specialized tooling when needed—maybe for specific projects or to suit your personal needs and forging style. The tools in this section are all fairly basic, but with them you can create a huge variety of work, including the projects in the next section (see page 120). The forging processes used to make these tools are simple—mainly various forms of taper. The new skill you will be learning is a process of heat treating to harden the working ends. You may wish to review "Metallurgy" chapter (see page 28) before beginning these projects.

Tools Project 1:

Chisel

A chisel is a useful tool for cutting and splitting hot metal and marking it cold. There are many different profile shapes that cut and shape slightly differently. The profile we will be making is simple and general purpose, but you may find you prefer a slightly different shape as you learn to use this tool.

Techniques involved: Billed taper, middle taper, forging hexagonal, heat treating

Goals: Learn to recognize heat colors.

Material: For the chisel to work, the cutting edge needs to be hardened so it maintains its sharpness to mark or cut other material. That means you must use hardenable material, a tool steel, or—to keep it simple—anything with a high-carbon content. Blacksmiths often use scrap material (see page 28), which is usually a simple high-carbon steel and is cheaper than purchasing tool steel. For this project, I am using 6 inches (15 cm) of ¾-inch (2cm) thick round drill rod, used in the oil-drilling industry, which I can purchase from my local supplier. Other sizes and shapes are viable, so use what you can find and adjust the directions accordingly.

FORGING

Any high-carbon steel is going to be literally harder to hammer than mild steel (as in it takes more effort to move it the same amount). This means it is more important than ever to get your material *hot* hot and to make sure it is heated all the way through.

1. Place about 1 inch (2.5 cm) of your material on the face of your anvil, and hammer it square. (1)

   Hold your material as still as possible, so each new face forged is the same length.

2. Rotate so the corners are now on the face of the anvil, and hammer them down until you have an octagon. (2)

   This is the struck end of the tool. Forging it into an octagon helps keep it cleaner and less prone to mushrooming over time.

Tip: *I used to make messy tools with just the most basic shapes to get the job done, but over time I have discovered that nice-looking, clean tools lead to better work and are simply more satisfying to use. It is worth taking a little extra time to make well-designed and well-forged tools.*

3. Heat the other end of the material and forge it into a billed taper. (3)

   This should not be a super-thin taper. It should be wide at the end, again, without getting too thin.

1

2

3

4

5

The next step is to flatten the middle of the tool and forge a slight taper from the middle out to either end. This step is functional, but it also improves the overall design. The flat face you will form in the middle of the tool should be opposite to the flat face of the billed taper. This helps you orient the blade of the chisel both visually and tactilely. Also, in tools that do not have a billed taper, it ensures that the tool will not roll off your anvil.

You can hold your material by either end for this step, but it is easier to accurately orient the flat plane to the bill if you can hold it by the billed taper.

4. Making sure your billed taper is oriented with the thin edge up, place the middle of your tool on the middle of the horn of the anvil, and hammer down. Hammer hardest in the center and lighten your blows as you move to either end. (4)
5. Rotate so the face that was up is now on the horn of the anvil, and hammer again.
6. Continue to forge as needed until you are happy with the result. There is no need to go too thin in the middle.
7. Flatten the tool on the face of the anvil, if needed. (5)
8. Set the tool aside, preferably on a neutral surface like a fire brick, and let it cool in the air until it is safe to touch.

   Letting the tool cool slowly in the air is a rough form of annealing the material and relieving any stresses left by the forging process. Setting it on a metal surface will cool the tool faster but more unevenly. This is likely overkill for simple high-carbon steel, but it is easy to do, so I do it.

HEAT TREATING

In these next steps, you will not be shaping the metal; you will be hardening and tempering it. We want a tool that is hard at the working end, so it cuts and marks steel effectively, but is soft on the struck end, where it is hit with the hammer—your hammer face is hardened, and hitting two hardened surfaces together can result in one or the other chipping at the edges. Not only could this ruin a tool, but the fragment that chips off will be sharp and moving quickly, so it could cause an injury.

1. Using a belt sander or grinder, shape the cutting edge of your tool. (6)

   The cutting edge should be almost flat, with a slight curve up at either end, then it must be beveled so that it becomes sharp, like the blade of a knife.

2. Grind or sand the scale off the faces of the chisel for 3–4 inches (7.5–10 cm). You need bright steel to be able to see the temper colors. (7)

3. Place about 2 inches (5 cm) or less of the chisel end of the tool in the forge and let it heat to above its transition temperature (see page 28).

Next, you will be both hardening and tempering your tool at the same time. Keep in mind that the process I am outlining is very rough. Tools like knives and anything made of alloy steels require much more control and precision. This is a quick and dirty method that will achieve serviceable results for these tools.

4. Remove the tool from the heat and dip about ½ inch (1.3 cm) of the end into your quench bucket, holding it in for several seconds. (8)

6

7

8

9

10

5. As quickly as possible, remove the tool from the water and scrub the surface to remove the scale. (9)

Tip: *You can use a grinding disk or file to scrub the scale off the surface. The best tool I have found is a broken piece of the grinding wheel from a pedestal grinder. Your hand will be close to sharp, hot metal, so wear a glove.*

6. Watch closely for the temper colors. Dip the tool again when the end is a straw yellow. (10)

   Using temper colors can be arbitrary (see page 29), but it is the method used by smiths for many years before more precise temperature indicators were invented. If you are doing this alone without a more experienced smith to guide you, the process will be one of trial and error. Do the best you can on the first round and remember that you can always heat treat again if you feel you have not achieved adequate hardness.

7. Repeat this process of quenching and cleaning the tool at least three times, or until the tool has cooled enough that the colors do not continue to change. You will be quenching very quickly at first, slowing down as the tool cools and the colors move slower and slower. (11)

8. Set the tool aside on a neutral surface and let it cool until it is safe to touch. (12)

   Even if it is hardened and tempered perfectly, your chisel will dull with use. You can always bring it back to the grinder or belt sander to sharpen it again.

   Once your chisel is cool, test the edge by hammering it into a piece of mild steel. It should make a cut mark in the metal, while the edge of the tool remains sharp. If it does not stay sharp, you may want to repeat the heat treating process.

11

12

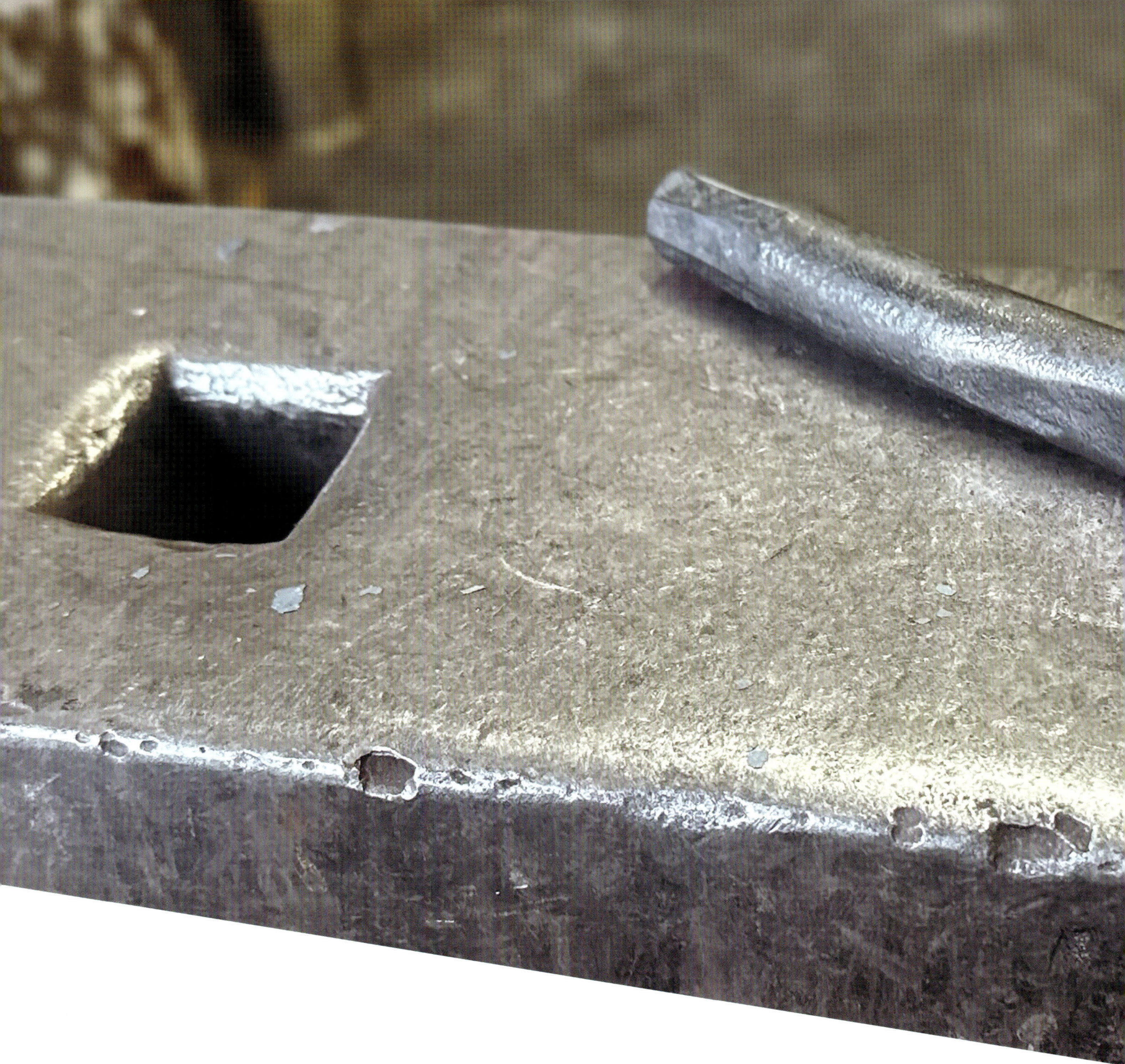

Tools Project 2:

Slot Punch

The steps for this tool and the next are almost identical to the chisel (see page 98); the only difference is the shape of the working end of the tool (the end that is not hit with a hammer). A slot punch works a bit like a hole punch, cutting a rectagonal hole through your material. Another tool, called a drift, is then hammered through that slot to form the final shape of the hole. You will make several drifts later in this chapter (see page 112).

Techniques involved: Flat pointed taper, middle taper, forging hexagonal, forging to precise size, heat treating

Goals: Learn to recognize heat colors.

Material: As with the chisel, this tool must be made from high-carbon steel. Again, I used 6 inches of ¾-inch (2cm) round drill rod.

FORGING

1. Forge the hexagon on the struck end of the tool. (1)

   The slot punch is not a completed pointed taper with a rectangular end. The final shape of the end of the tool can be refined using a grinder, but the goal is to forge it to a rectangle that is 5⁄16 inches (0.8 cm) long by 1⁄8 inch (0.4 cm) wide. It is common to have multiple slot punches to form different-sized holes, but this size is multipurpose enough for the projects in the following section.

2. Forge the working end of the tool to an unfinished pointed taper with a rectangular end. (2)

3. Forge the middle taper, making sure that the flat of the middle is on the same face as the short width of the end of the punch. (3)

4. Let the tool cool on a neutral surface.

1

2

3

4

5

6

HEAT TREATING

Again, these steps are the same as with the chisel (see page 102), but I will repeat them briefly as a reminder.

1. Once the tool is cool, grind, sand, or file the end to shape and clean the faces to bright metal.

   Again, the end of this tool should be 5/16 inch (0.8 cm) long, 1/8 inch (0.4 cm) wide, flat on the end, and sharp on all edges. It works like a hole punch, so every edge is a cutting edge. (4)

2. Heat the working end in the forge to above the transition temperature.

3. Dip about ½–¾ inch (1.3–2 cm) into the quench bucket for several seconds.

4. Bring it out, scrub the surface, and quench again when the tip is straw yellow. (5)

5. Repeat the quenching process until the colors no longer change. (6)

6. Set the tool aside on a neutral surface to cool in air.

Tools Project 3:

Round Punch

The only difference between this tool, the chisel, and the slot punch is the working end of the tool. This one is even more like a hole punch because it is round. Generally, this tool is used without a drift to make a hole through thinner material.

Techniques involved: Round taper, middle taper, forging hexagonal, forging to precise size, heat treating

Goals: Learn to recognize heat colors.

Material: This tool must be made from high-carbon steel. I used 6 inches (15 cm) of ¾-inch (2cm) round drill rod.

FORGING

1. Forge the hexagon on the struck end of the tool.

   The round punch is an incomplete pointed taper with a round end. The final shape of the end of the tool can be refined using a grinder, but the goal is for it to be a circle about ¼ inch (0.6 cm) in diameter. Of course, you can make round punches of different sizes as you need them.

2. Forge the working end of the tool to a square unfinished pointed taper that is about ¼ inch (0.6 cm) wide.

3. Forge the edges of the square down to form an octagonal taper.

4. Continue forging the taper to a clean round. (1)

5. Forge the middle taper. (2)

   A circle does not have faces, of course, so for this tool it does not matter how the middle flat is oriented.

6. Let the tool cool on a neutral surface.

1

2

3

4

5

HEAT TREATING

These are the same simplified steps as for the slot punch (see page 107). For detailed steps, refer to the chisel project (see page 102).

1. Once the tool is cool, grind the end to shape and clean the faces to bright metal. (3)
2. As with the slot punch, the end of this tool must be flat and the edges sharp.
3. Heat the end in the forge to above the transition temperature.

   Dip about ½–¾ inch (1.3–2 cm) into the quench bucket for several seconds.
4. Bring it out, scrub the surface, and quench again when the tip is straw yellow. (4)
5. Repeat the quenching process until the colors no longer draw. (5)
6. Set the tool aside to cool on a neutral surface.

Tools Project 4:

Drift

Drifts are tools that are hammered through a hole made by a slot punch (see page 104) to form a specifically sized and shaped pass-through. Drifts can be quite large for forming something such as the eye of a hammer, or smaller for simple joinery, which is what we will be making. They can be any size or shape that is needed, but the most common is round, with square a close second. We will be making two drifts that will be used for projects in the next section.

Techniques involved: Tapering, maintaining precise size

Goals: Make drifts of specific sizes and shapes.

Material: Drifts shape metal by passing through it, not being hammered into it, so they don't need to be made of high-carbon steel. That said, you certainly could use high carbon if you want.

For ⅜-inch (1cm) round drift: 4 inches (10 cm) of ⅜-inch (1cm) round mild steel
For ⅜-inch (1cm) square drift: 4 inches (10 cm) of ⅜-inch (1cm) square mild steel

ROUND DRIFT

1. Forge a hexagon on about ½ inch (1.3 cm) of the struck end of the tool. (1)

   In this case, the hexagon is extra-important. It needs to be smaller than the ⅜-inch (1cm) diameter of the tool, so that the tool easily passes through.

2. Forge a flat taper on the other end of the tool, being careful to keep about ¾ inch (2 cm) of the material unforged so it maintains its diameter. (2)

3. Using a grinder, belt sander, or file, clean the flat faces of the tool and remove any mill scale. (3)

   The cleaner the tool, the easier it will pass through the slot, but be sure not to remove material from the unforged part of the drift. You want it to stay at the ⅜-inch (1cm) dimension.

1

2

3

4

5

6

SQUARE DRIFT

1. Forge the hexagon on the struck end, again making sure it is smaller than the diameter of the body of the material. (4)
2. Forge a billed taper on the other end of the tool. (5)
3. Grind or sand in the same way as for the round drift. (6)

Using these same steps, you can make any size of drifts you want, but you will need these two for later projects. Drifts can get bent in the process of using them. If this happens, they can easily be straightened cold on the anvil.

Tools Project 5:

Monkey Tool

A monkey tool is very simple and highly useful. It is placed over a tenon and hammered into the shoulder of the tenon to make it clean and square. You will be making tenons for the freestanding double hooks project (see page 142).

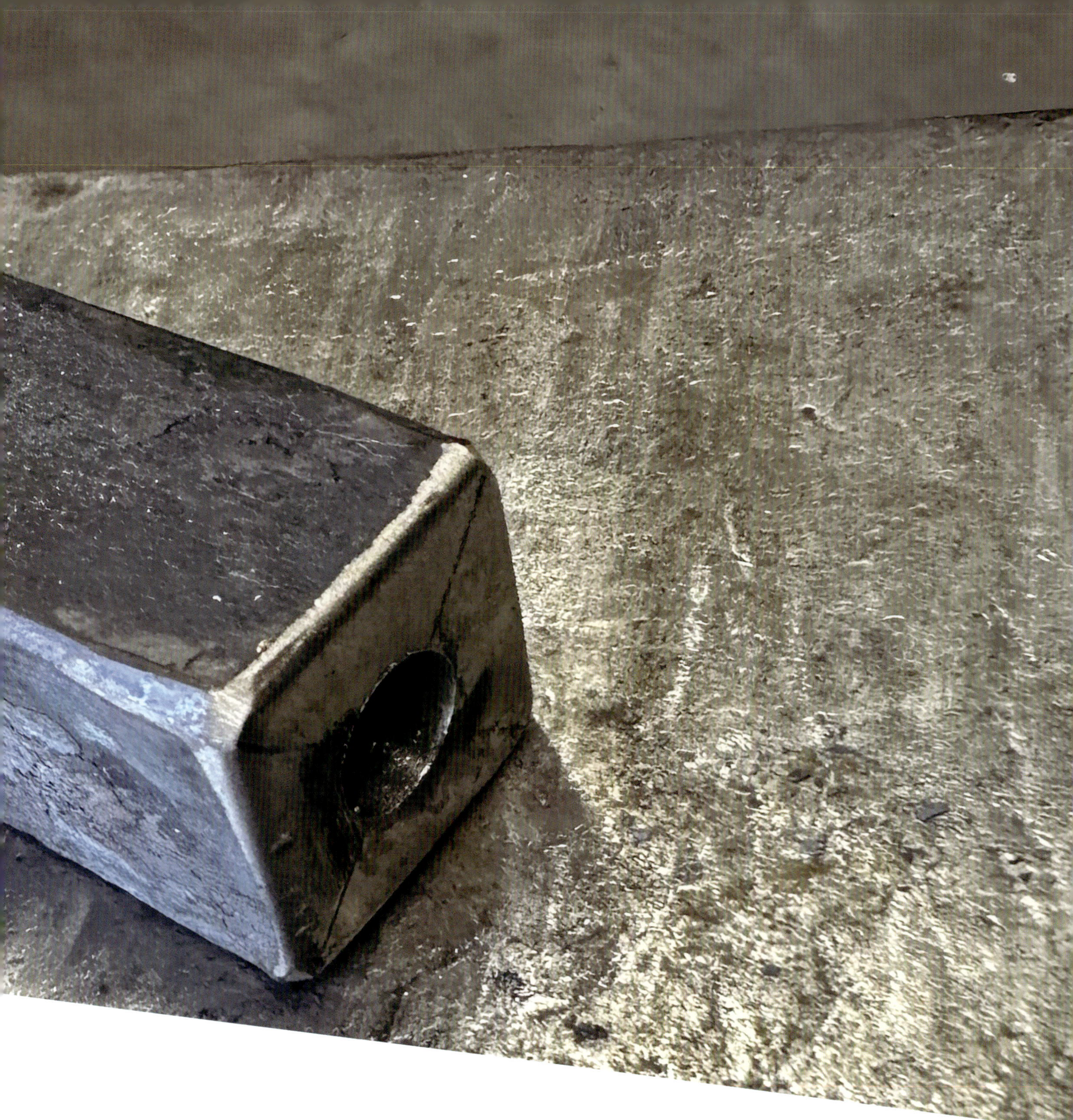

Techniques involved: Drilling

Goals: Make a tool for cleaning up tenons.

Material: This tool does not need to be made from a high-carbon steel; mild steel will work just fine. You can use square or round, though square will be easier. The base of the tool needs to be larger than the material the tenon is made from, so it can vary depending on the project. Larger is better, though, since it makes the tool heavier and less likely to bend. For this project, I am using 5 inches (12.7 cm) of ¾-inch (2cm) square mild steel.

1. Forge a hexagon on one end of the tool. (1)

   This is for the same reason you forge a hexagon on the end of the chisel and drifts.

2. Let the tool cool in air.

   Since this is mild steel quenching in water shouldn't technically harden it, but in my experience it can make it difficult to drill into. So its safer to let it cool in air, even though it takes longer.

3. Using a center punch, mark the middle of the end face of the material opposite the side with the hexagon. (2)

   If you are using square material, just draw straight lines from one corner to the opposite, forming an X. Where the lines intersect is the middle of the material. Marking with a center punch is important to keep the drill bit centered.

4. Mark the middle of one side of the tool, about 1½ inches (3.8 cm) up from the non-hexagonal end.

   You will be drilling a hole here as a relief to let air and scale escape when the tool is being used. This helps make sure the tool doesn't get stuck on the tenon.

1

2

3

4

5. Drill the hole in the end of the tool, slightly larger than the size of the tenon you are using the tool on. (3)

In the next section, you will be making a 3/8-inch (1cm) tenon from ½-inch (1.3cm) round stock, so you need a drill bit of at least 3/8 inch (1 cm) or slightly larger. Something like 25/64 inch (0.9 cm) would be good. If you go too large, you will not get a clean base for the tenon, and it will not fit the pass-through.

The depth of the hole should accommodate the length of whatever tenon you will be using it on, and should intersect with the relief hole. I recommend a depth of about 2 inches (5 cm), even though this is much longer than you will need for the specific project we will be using it on.

I have a drill press and a vice to hold material while I am drilling it. If you have only a hand drill, you can use that, but be extra careful to keep the bit perpendicular to the end of the tool.

6. Drill the second hole in the side of the tool. (4)

You can use the same size of drill bit as the first hole, but anything larger than ¼ inch (0.6 cm) should do. The hole can go all the way through the tool, or just through until it intersects with the vertical hole.

TOOL USE AND JOINERY

One of the great advantages of being a blacksmith is the ability to make your own tools. Not only does it teach you a lot about forging and metallurgy, but you can also invent specialized tooling when needed—maybe for specific projects or to suit your personal needs and forging style. The tools in this section are all fairly basic, but with them, you can create a huge variety of work, including the projects in the next section. The forging processes used to make these tools are simple, mainly various forms of tapers. The new skill you will be learning is a process of heat treating to harden the working ends. You may wish to review the "Metallurgy" chapter (see page 27) before beginning these projects.

Tool Use and Joinery Project 1:

J hook

This simple hook can be made quickly by using the techniques you have been practicing. The new challenge will be using your round punch (see page 108) to make two holes to hang the hook with. As your first project using your tools, it will be basic and straightforward, allowing you to develop and practice the process of punching to be implemented in more complicated projects later.

Techniques involved: Holding tongs, using a round punch

Goals: Familiarizing yourself with the use of a punch. This means holding and placing the punch itself, hammering it into the metal, cooling it as necessary, and holding your material without using your hands.

Material: You can use round, square, or even flat material for this project. I recommend nothing smaller than ⅜ inch (1 cm). For this example, I am using 7 inches (17.8 cm) of ½-inch (1.3cm) round bar.

HOW TO HOLD YOUR TONGS

You will need two hands to use your punch: one to hold it with and one to hammer it. This means you need to figure out how to hold your material without your hands. The most common solution is to hold it with your legs. To do that, you need a way for the tongs to stay tight on the material without your hand squeezing them closed. This can be accomplished using a tong collar.

A tong collar is a simple oval of metal—most of mine are made with ¼-inch (0.6cm) round bar. To use a tong collar, grab your material with your tongs as you usually would, squeeze the reins together, then slip the collar on the reins with your other hand. If the collar is sized correctly, there will be enough tension in the tongs to hold the collar in place, and the collar will hold the tongs closed on your material. I use tong collars often—even when I don't need an extra hand—and have several sizes readily available. (1)

Once your material is safely held, remove it from the forge, set it on your anvil, and hold the ends of the tongs with your legs. There are many ways to do this, depending on your height, the height of the anvil, your body, and so on, but I will describe two common options.

The first option would be to hold the tongs between your legs (kind of like you have to go to the bathroom badly!). This only works if you and your anvil are at the right height for the material to remain flat on the face of the anvil when held like this.

The second option, and the way I usually do it, is to tuck the reins into the front crease of my hip, on the same side as my hammer hand (my right). I lift my right heel so I am on my toes, giving the reins a bit of a shelf to rest on. This is undoubtedly a tricky move to make, and it will take practice. You will have to figure out what works best with your body and your forging setup. (2a, 2b)

There are ways other than those I've described. Experiment, research, and problem solve to find your preferred method. Many people use an adjustable stand to hold their tongs, or you could forge with a friend and have them hold your material for you. Whatever method you use, you will be slow at first but will get faster and smoother with time.

1

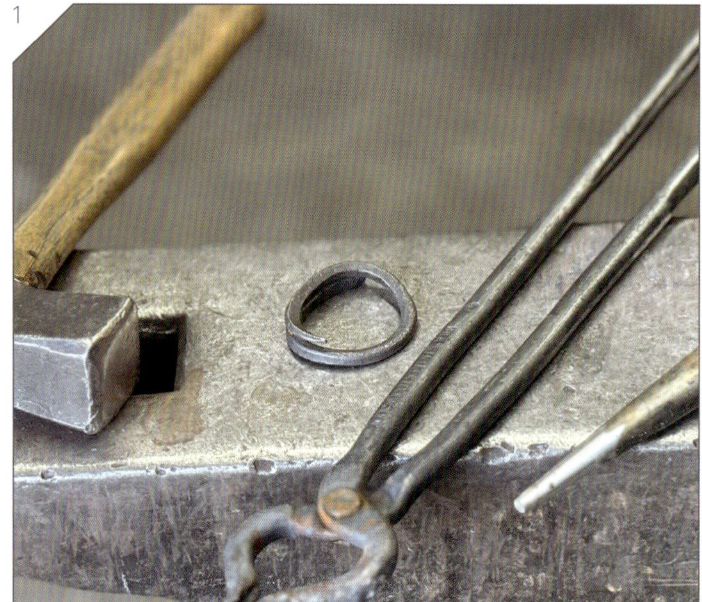

2a

2b

3

4

HOW TO USE A PUNCH

As you know, your punch is made from higher carbon steel, meaning it should maintain its sharp edges and shape. But if it is heated too much, even just by touching hot metal, it will deform. So, as you use your punch, you will need to cool it often. I use a small container of water that sits on my anvil stand in front of me (3). You could move your quench bucket close to you, place your water on top of the anvil, or add a special holder to your stand for this purpose.

There is a rhythm to this process, and, as with everything, it will be tricky at first and get easier with time. The following are detailed steps for using any kind of punch. The steps for the hook start later (see page 126).

1. Place your material on the anvil and hold it with your legs, using your preferred method
2. Pick up the punch in your non-dominant hand and place it in the proper location on your material. You can pre-mark your material by using a center punch or just eyeball it.
3. Hammer the punch into the material for four to six blows.
4. Rest your hammer on the face of the anvil. Dip your punch in the water.
5. Place your punch back into the hole you have started, and repeat the process. If your metal is not hot enough, place it back in the forge and repeat Steps 1–4.
6. When you can tell that you have cut through the material, move the area with the hole over the pritchel hole and hammer your punch all the way through it. (4)

You may be able to do two or three rounds of hammering before your material cools, or you may only get a few hits in. With thinner material, you will eventually be able to punch through in one heat. With thicker material, you will want to punch from both sides.

The slot and round punches work like a hole punch, using sharp edges to cut into and through the material and removing a small piece of metal called a "slug." On thicker material, and if your punch is nice and sharp, you may not need to use the pritchel hole; you can knock the slug out on the face of the anvil. When using a slot punch, the next step is to reheat your metal and hammer a drift through the hole, but with a round punch you are creating the size and shape of the hole you want in one step.

1. Forge the hook end of the hook.

   You can do this simply with a taper or add a finial. A ball end is a nice addition if this will be a coat or clothes hook. For this example, I forged a billed taper, lengthening my material to 8½ inches (21.6 cm) and then bending it around the horn. (5)

2. Place about 1 inch (2.5 cm) of the unforged end on the face of the anvil, with the hook of the anvil facing the floor. (6)

5

6

7

8

3. Hammer the material on the face of the anvil down to form a flattened surface. Turn it on its side to clean up the edges. (7)

   The result should be a flat area with a clean transition into the body of the hook. This transition will only be clean if you keep your material in the same place on the edge of the anvil. The first few hammer blows flatten the material enough to create a difference in the thickness of the material on and off the face of the anvil. The thickness of the unhammered area can be used to register the material tightly against the edge of the anvil.

The next step is to punch two holes, using your round punch (see page 125).

4. Punch two holes in the flat section you just forged. They should be far enough apart to accommodate the heads of two screws. (8)

   Your hook is now complete.

Tool Use and Joinery Project 2:

Bottle Opener

A bottle opener is a fun object to make because it has a function, but there is a lot of room for interesting decorative and design decisions. I am going to walk you through a simple bottle opener and offer some thoughts and suggestions for changes to add to other openers.

Techniques involved: Using a slot punch, drifting

Goals: Improving punching and drifting technique; developing use of the horn

Material: As with most of these projects, you can use material of various sizes. The example I am showing you is easier because it is made out of thin material. I used 6¼ inches (16 cm) of ¼ x ⅞-inch (0.6 x 2.2cm) flat bar.

Your first step will be to punch and drift a hole. In this case, you will use a slot punch to make the initial hole, then drift it with your round punch (see page 125).

1. Forge a taper on one end of your material.

   This is only a design element; it is not necessary for the function of the opener.

2. Punch a hole in the other end of your material with your slot punch. (1)

   The farthest edge of your punch should be about ½ inch (1.3 cm) from the edge of your material. You can either eyeball this or mark it with a center punch.

3. Reheat the metal and place the slot over the pritchel hole.

4. Holding your tongs with your legs, place the tapered end of your drift into the slot. Hammer it down and through the pritchel hole. (2a, 2b)

Tip: *Eventually, you will be able to hammer the drift all the way through thin material like this in a single heat, but in the beginning it may take several attempts. If you see that your metal is cool around the punch, simply flip it over, place the struck end into the pritchel hole, and tap it out of your material. You will then need to reheat and repeat the process. Using tongs, pick up your drift and cool it before using it again.*

1

2a

2b

3

4

5

Your next stage will be to enlarge the hole until it is about 1 × 7/8 inches (2.5 x 2.2 cm) deep. It must be wide enough to be larger than a standard bottle cap, and just deep enough to provide leverage to open the bottle. If you want, you could make a larger drift than 3/8 inch (1 cm), possibly ½ inch (1.3 cm). This will make it easier to fit the hole over the horn and will give you a head start on the stretching process.

5. Place the hole you just made over the end of your horn, so the point of the horn is inside the drifted hole.

6. Begin hammering the outside edge of the material, starting with the corners at the end of the flat bar. (3)

   This is an instance where your metal must be *hot* hot. If it is only hot, the points will bend and fold into the rest of the material. If it is *hot* hot, they will squish back into the material.

7. Once one corner is hammered in, reheat your material and flip it so the other corner is pointing up. Hammer it in as well.

   Remember that the outside edge of the horn is at an angle. Keep your material angled slightly toward you so the inside of the hole retains a right angle. (4)

8. Continue hammering the outside edge until you have a round hole that is about 1 inch (2.5 cm) in diameter. (5)

Tip: *Be sure to hammer evenly, angling your tongs up and down so the whole outside band maintains the same thickness. Also, continue to flip the side of the material that faces in, so you can hammer completely around the outside band. You can even change your position, so you are standing on the other side of the horn, in order to make sure everything is forged evenly. Hammer carefully—you can always make the hole larger but you can't shrink it.*

Once the hole is slightly larger than 1 inch (2.5 cm) in diameter, it must be squished to an oval.

9. Place one shoulder where the handle meets the circle over the far edge of the anvil, and tap the circle in toward you. (6)

10. Repeat with the other shoulder. The finished oval should be about 1 inch (2.5 cm) wide by 7/8 inch (2.2 cm) tall. (7)

The last step is to make the lip on the inside edge that goes under the bottle cap to leverage it up. You can do this with a top tool, if you have one, or just use your anvil.

11. Place the inside edge of the hole, nearest the handle of the bottle opener, on the very tip of your horn. Hammer it down to pull out a small circle of material. (8a–c)

6

7

8a

8b

That's it for the functional aspects of this piece. Finishing the handle is up to you! In this sample, I just forged a little scroll. (9)

You can add any of the twists or finials that have been covered previously, or come up with something new. Try making this bottle opener from different-sized material, such as square or round stock, to accommodate alternative designs.

8c

9

Tool Use and Joinery Project 3:

Wall-Mounted Hook Set

Once you have made this hook set, you will see that there are many fun and interesting design changes you can make to it. I hope this will be a project you can enjoy adapting multiple times. For the first time we will be keeping things simple, but, as always, feel free to make changes at any point.

Techniques involved: Punching, drifting, riveting, forging a repeated shape

Goals: Correctly lay out the positions of multiple holes to punch and drift, think through and plan for functionality of the project, and forge three pieces of the same size and shape.

Material: The following measurements were used for the example in the photographs:

Hooks: Three pieces at 3½ inches (9 cm) of ⅜ inch (1 cm) round
Backing piece: 16 inches (41 cm) of ½ inch (1.3 cm) square
Rivets: Three rivets at ⅜-inch (1 cm) diameter and ¾ inch (2 cm) long
Lag bolts: Two ⅜-inch (1 cm) lag bolts at 1½ inches (3.8 cm) long

HOOKS

The challenge here is to make three pieces that are the same size and shape. I have found that the best way to do this is to forge all the shapes at the same time (complete Step 1 for all three hooks, then Step 2 for all three, and so on). Your body will remember the movements you just made and will replicate them the second and third time.

These hooks are very similar to the J hook (see page 122); the only difference is that they are smaller, and you only need to punch one hole in each.

1. Taper one end of each of the three pieces. (1)

   I chose a billed taper, but any will work; you can even do some fun and fancy finials. Keep in mind the use of these hooks and avoid anything with a sharp end that would damage clothing, if that is what you intend to use these for.

2. Heat the other end and flatten about ½ inch (1.3 cm), in the same way as for the single J hook (see page 127).

   Repeat for the other two hooks. (2)

3. Use your round punch to make a hole in the flattened end of each of the hooks. (3)

4. Heat the tapered ends again and curve each one over the horn.

1

2

3

4

5

5. Compare the curves of the three hooks and adjust as necessary until they are the same. (4)

BACKING PIECE

The layout will have to be done before any forging. You will need one hole for each of the hooks, plus two more to hang the complete piece on a wall, so you need to punch and drift five ⅜-inch (1cm) holes. The three hooks should be grouped around the middle, and the bolt holes should be toward the ends. In this design, the middle of the backing piece comes off the wall in a curve to accommodate the backs of the rivets, so the piece can sit flush to the wall.

When you mark for a hole, remember that the end of your tool is a rectangle, not a point. I make two marks with my center punch: one to line up the top of the tool, the other for the bottom. For ½-inch (1.3cm) material, you will punch from both sides, so be sure the marks are the same on either side. You also need to mark where the bend will occur. You can use a center punch or a chisel line for this. This mark should only be on one side (what will end up being the wall side of the piece). My layout for this project is as follows.

6. Mark for a hole at 1½ inches (3.8 cm) from each end.
7. Mark for one hole in the middle.
8. Mark for one hole 3 inches (7.5 cm) from the center on each side.
9. Mark for a bend 3 inches (7.5 cm) from each end. (5)

Next, you will be punching and drifting each hole.

10. Position the slot punch parallel in the middle of the material, lined up with your marks.
11. Hit four to six times, being especially careful with the first few hits to make sure your tool is in the correct location.
12. Cool the tool and continue to hammer until the material needs to be reheated.
13. Punch from the other side. You have your marks to guide you, but you should also be able to see where the tool is coming through, based on the way the material is moving around it.
14. Punch from both sides until you meet in the middle and punch out the slug. If your tool is sharp and everything is lined up correctly, the slug will come out cleanly without the need to move to the pritchel hole. If the slug is more difficult to get out, move over the pritchel hole and hammer your slot punch in until the slug is removed. Be sure to keep your tool cool and sharpen it often.

15. Punch and drift each hole, moving from one end of the material to the other. (6)

16. Taper the 1 inch (2.5 cm) of material after the hole on each end. (7)

I have done a billed taper to match the hooks. Next you will make the bends and curve the middle.

17. Hold the material with the bend mark up and just off the edge of the anvil farthest from you.

18. Gently hammer that leg down to less than a 90-degree angle. (8) The greater the angle, the more the backing piece will sit off the wall.

    The goal is to have a clean bend, not a curve. To achieve this, move back and forth between hammering the leg down and flattening the part that remains on the anvil. When hammering the leg down, your blows should be right at the edge of the anvil and scooping slightly back up toward yourself, as if you are pulling the material up into the corner.

    When hammering the material on top of the anvil, your blows can glance slightly away from yourself to push the material the other way into the bend. None of your blows should hit hard directly into the side or face of the anvil, since this will thin the material rather than bend it.

6

7

8

9

19. Repeat this step on the other end of the material. (9)

20. Using the horn, gently curve the middle section until the two legs are in the same plane. (10a, 10b)

The material will be thinner and want to bend more sharply where the holes are. Keep this in mind and hammer gently to make an even bend.

10a

10b

RIVETING

Once your material is cool, the final stage is to rivet the hooks to the backing piece.

21. Place a hook over one of the holes and put a rivet through both pieces.

    Each side of the rivet will look different once completed. I chose the manufactured head to be on the outside.

22. Flip the material so the manufactured rivet head is against the face of the anvil. Ensure the hook is lined up correctly. (11)

23. Starting with heavy blows directly down, begin to hammer the back of the rivet.

24. Watch how the rivet is deforming, and adjust your blows accordingly, changing the angle to spread the back of the rivet out. Make sure it is not just bending over.

25. Continue hammering until the back of the rivet is spread enough to secure the hook.

Tip: *You can heat the rivet instead of hammering it cold. You could do this with a torch while it is in place, or heat the rivet in the forge and quickly move it into place before it cools. If you have the right technique, this is not strictly necessary. You also may find a slightly longer rivet easier to make the hooks secure, but the risk of it bending rather than deforming is greater.*

11

26. Repeat the riveting steps for all three hooks, and you are done. (12)

    In these photos I am again using lags that I forged square. Feel free to use whatever you think looks best. If you do decide to forge your own, remember that the zinc coating on a lot of hardware is very toxic when heated. (13)

12

13

Tool Use and Joinery Project 4:

Freestanding Double Hooks

This is another project with multiple pieces that fit together. You will be making tenons for the first time, using the monkey tool you made earlier (see page 116). This project has free-moving pieces in the form of two swiveling hooks—it's always fun to have pieces that move! Use the hooks to hang potted plants, a bird feeder, a solar lantern, or anything else that you come up with.

Techniques involved: Punching and drifting round material, making tenons, repeating the same shape

Goals: Forge and rivet your first tenons.

Material: To add an extra challenge, I am using round material for the body and crossbar of this piece. As far as size goes, the longer the body, the taller the finished project will be; the longer the crosspiece, the larger the objects that can be hung from it. For this example, I will be forging on a small scale to keep things simple.

Body: 27 inches (69 cm) of ½-inch (1.3cm) round.
Crosspiece: 15 inches (38 cm) of ½-inch (1.3cm) round
Leg: 5 inches (12.7 cm) of ½-inch (1.3cm) round
Hooks: Two pieces of 6 inches (15 cm) of ½-inch (1.3cm) round

HOOKS

These pieces are the easiest, so we'll start here. As with the wall-mounted hook set (see page 134), the goal is for these pieces to be the same shape, which means forging them at the same time—complete one step for one hook, then do the same for the other. We will be forging a ball on the top of these hooks, which will allow them to swivel in the crosspiece. The process is the same as the ball end finial (see pages 92–94).

1. Following the steps for the ball end finial, forge a ball on the end of each piece of hook material. (1)
2. Hold the ball over the far edge of the anvil and begin to forge down the neck and the body of the hook.
3. Flip the material when needed to hold by the ball end, so you can dimension the full length of the material down to ¼-inch (0.6 cm) diameter. (2a, b)

   When dimensioning material, remember to forge square first, then knock the corners off to bring it back to round.

1

2a

2b

3

4

4. Curve each hook to the desired shape around the horn and adjust as needed. (3)

CROSSPIECE

You will be punching three $\frac{3}{8}$-inch (1cm) holes in this piece: one in the middle to attach it to the body, and one at each end for the hooks. The added difficulty here will be that you are using round instead of square material. This means that when you are doing the layout, you can only mark one side. But after the first round or two of using the punch, you should be able to see exactly where it is coming through to position your punch from the other side. Be careful to mark the hole locations on the same plane. I marked the holes for the hooks at 1 inch (2.5 cm) from each end.

5. Use your slot punch and $\frac{3}{8}$-inch (1cm) drift to punch and drift all three holes.

   You may want to add a little forged texture to this piece between the holes—that is up to you.

BODY

This piece has a pointed taper on one end, one punched and drifted hole, and a round tenon on the other end. We will start at the easy end and move up to the tenon.

6. Mark, then punch and drift a square $\frac{3}{8}$-inch (1cm) hole at 4 inches (10 cm) from one end of the piece.

   We are using a square drift in this case because we do not want the leg to rotate in the hole. Be careful to line up the drift so it is parallel with the sides of your material.

7. Forge the end after the hole to a pointed taper. It should be 5–6 inches (12.7–15 cm) long. (4)

This point will be driven into the ground up to the hole to hold the piece upright. The longer this taper, the more stability the piece will have. If you are using a long piece for the body, this leg should be longer. Pass the entire body piece through the forge and add texture if you want.

The next steps are to tenon the other end of this piece. A tenon is a smaller diameter section of material on the end of a larger diameter piece. It can pass through a hole and be riveted to create a joint, which is what we will be doing. We want this joint to be tight, and the riveted head of the tenon to look nice. The key to achieving this is a tenon of the right length and diameter. The length can be forged long and cut, but you must be careful with your hammering to make sure you do not make the tenon too small.

8. While your material is cold, use your chisel to mark all the way around at 1 inch (2.5 cm) from the end.

   Treat the material as if it were square, focusing on creating chisel marks on all four "sides." Then mark the "corners" until your line is all the way around.

9. Heat your material and forge this mark in. (5)

   Remember to cool your chisel periodically. Don't forge the marks too deep. If you do, you will cut through or weaken your material.

10. Place the 1 inch (2.5 cm) of material you have marked off on the face of your anvil, with the chisel mark right on the edge.

    Choose an area where the radius of the corner is somewhat sharp.

11. Hammer directly down into the face of the anvil, creating a step where the material changes from round and thicker to flat and thinner.

12. Rotate the material to forge the other "side" flat, making sure to stay in line with the step you just created. (6)

    You are creating a transition in a similar way as with forging a ball end, just opposite. You want to be as precise with your hammer blows as possible, so you have an even step all the way around. The goal is to forge up to the chisel line but not hit anywhere on the other side.

13. Continue to rotate until all four "sides" are forged flat and about 3/8 inch (1 cm) wide, then forge down the "corners" and bring the tenon back to round.

    Forge carefully. You can always make the tenon smaller, but you can't make it bigger. If you aren't happy with it, you can cut it off and try again. Your body piece will just be a little shorter.

14. Heat the tenon again, making sure about 1 inch (2.5 cm) of the body of the material is hot as well.

15. Place your monkey tool on the end of the tenon and hammer it toward you. (7)

5

6

7

8

9

10

16. Repeat this step as necessary until you are happy with the result. (8)

    If you heat too much of the body, you will forge curves in it instead of shaping the shoulder, so be aware of how much material is being heated. You can also isolate the heat by pouring water over the piece to cool it almost up to the tenon. The point of the monkey tool is to create a clean shoulder for the tenon to sit against the material it passes through.

LEG

This piece will be tapered at one end and tenoned at another. The tenon will be square to fit the hole at the bottom of the body piece, then tapered and bent to create an upside-down L shape that will hold this piece upright. It will need some interesting forging in order to accomplish these goals.

17. Forge one end into a square taper.

    This will also lengthen your material. The longer the taper, the deeper the piece can go into the ground.

18. Using the same steps as above, forge a ⅜-inch (1cm) square tenon on the end. (9)

    We do not have a square monkey tool (it is possible to make one, but the process is more advanced than we can cover here), so take this as an opportunity to forge as cleanly and carefully as possible. If you happen to have access to any type of guillotine tool, it will aid in all your tenoning.

The next step is to forge a right-angle bend in the leg, with the goal of creating a clean sharp corner rather than a rounded one.

19. Hold the leg on the far edge of your anvil, with 2½ inches (6.4 cm) on the face of the anvil and the pointed taper hanging off .

    Be sure to position so the square tenon is in the same plane as the bend.

20. Hammer the pointed end down to a slight angle. (10)

21. Hammer at the bend on the side of the anvil in a scooping motion upward, as if you are pulling the corner toward you.

22. Hammer the bend on the face of the anvil in a pushing motion away from you.

    These hammer blows move the material into the corner, rather than squishing the material to be thinner.

23. Alternate between these hammer positions until you have a clean corner. Hammer the point down to a right angle. (11)

Forging a square corner is not entirely necessary for the functionality of the piece, but it is a valuable skill to learn, and this is a good place to practice it. More steps are needed to get a truly sharp corner, but this is a good start.

11

RIVETING THE TENON

First you must cut the tenon to the proper length.

24. Place the tenon through the square hole in the body piece and mark it at ⅜ inch (1 cm) from the outside edge of the hole. (12)

25. Cut the tenon at this mark.

Use a power tool or hot cut with your chisel (if you cut with your chisel, be sure not to hammer all the way through the tenon, so you are hammering your chisel into the face of your anvil). You should cut almost all the way through, then break the remainder off.

Tip: *For a nicer-looking rivet, you may want to do a little sanding or filing to clean up this cut end so it is flat with slightly rounded edges.*

12

26. Heat the tenon but as little of the body of the piece as possible.

Your goal is to forge the tenon into a rivet but not have the rest of the piece bend. If you have one, it will be cleaner to heat the end of the tenon with the torch while it is placed through the hole. If you are using a forge, you may need to quench the material in water so only the head of the tenon is hot.

27. Quickly place the tenon through the hole and begin to hammer the heated end down into a rivet.

The way you hold both pieces of material is important. The following photos show some examples, but you may find better ways that work with your specific setup. Test your holding and hammering positions with your material cold first to practice your moves. (13a, b, c)

13a

13b

13c

14

You will almost certainly not get the tenon properly set with the first heat, so you will need to reheat the whole section. Before you forge, be sure to thoroughly cool all the areas you do not want to move. If you have a vice, there are many ways you can clamp the material to make riveting easier, and a torch that will definitely simplify the process. However you get there, in the end you should have the leg connected to the body piece at a right angle, with minimal wiggle. Don't worry if this takes multiple tries; just remember the main principles of how hot metal moves, and work through the best way to get it to move where and how you want. (14)

If this method of attaching the leg is frustrating or seems not to work for you, there are other methods you can try. For example, forge and rivet the tenon before tapering and bending the leg piece. This allows you to set the unforged end of the leg on the face of the anvil and hammer against that to upset the tenon and create the joint. You will likely still need several heats to finish the joint and will have to be very careful about keeping the leg cool so it doesn't bend. You will then need to taper and bend the leg while it is attached to the body. This requires some creative holding positions but is doable.

ATTACHING THE CROSSPIECE

You will repeat the same tenon-riveting techniques for this joint that you just did for the leg (see page 148). The only difference is that you are working with a round tenon, and this joint will be easier to hold. The orientation of the crosspiece isn't important, but it looks nice and clean if it is in line with or perpendicular to the leg.

28. Cut the tenon to the appropriate length.
29. Heat the tenon and cool the body piece as necessary.
30. Place the crosspiece over the body piece and forge the tenon down to a riveted head. (15)
31. In this case, you are hammering against your own strength holding the body piece. There are many other ways you can hold your material to forge the tenon while keeping the crosspiece in place. (16a, b).
32. If you have a vice, I recommend clamping the body piece and holding the crosspiece with your hand. (17)

    As with the leg piece, it is likely you will not get the tenon set on the first heat. You can always reheat the area, cool what you don't want to move, and hammer some more. You may also find you can tighten the tenon more than you expect by hammering it cold.

33. Slip the hooks through the holes at the end of the crosspiece, and you are done. (18)

15

16a

16b

17

18

Tool Use and Joinery Project 4:

Potted Plant Hanger

The parts of this project are dry fit—there is no riveting and some pieces can come apart, like the freestanding double hooks (see page 142). This means that the pieces have to balance correctly, since they are not held in place with tension.

Techniques involved: Punching and drifting, repeating the same shape, forging precisely for balance, splitting with a chisel

Goals: Forging multiple pieces that fit together to create a balanced object

Material: The dimensions for this object can be adjusted to accommodate different-sized pots, but we will start with something (hopefully) easy to find. Small terra-cotta pots typically have a 4-inch (10cm) or 6-inch (15cm) diameter at the top. This example uses a 4-inch (10cm) pot.

Top hook: 4 inches (10 cm) of ½-inch (1.3cm) round bar
Side hooks: Two lengths of 3½ inches (8.9 cm) of ½-inch (1.3cm) round bar
Crosspiece: 6½ inches (16.5 cm) of ¼ x 1-inch (0.6 x 2.5cm) flat bar
Body: 8¾ inches (22.2 cm) of ¼ x 1-inch (0.6 x 2.5cm) flat bar

This project requires some mathematic reasoning to determine the length of material to use for the body piece. I have provided the measurements for a 4-inch (10cm) pot, but what if you want to use a different size? This will mean a different length of material for the body and crosspieces. Below are the steps you need to follow to figure out an alternative length, with explanations using the 4-inch (10cm) pot from the example.

1. Decide the dimensions of the object you want to forge—in this case, the body piece.

   The piece sits under the lip of the pot. When we measure, the width of this area of the pot is 3¾ inches (9.5 cm). So, we need a circle that is 3¾ inches (9.5 cm) on the inside diameter. We also need two tabs on either side for the hooks. I decided, based on my experience and instinct, what will look good and work well, that these tabs should be 1¼ inches (3.2 cm) long.

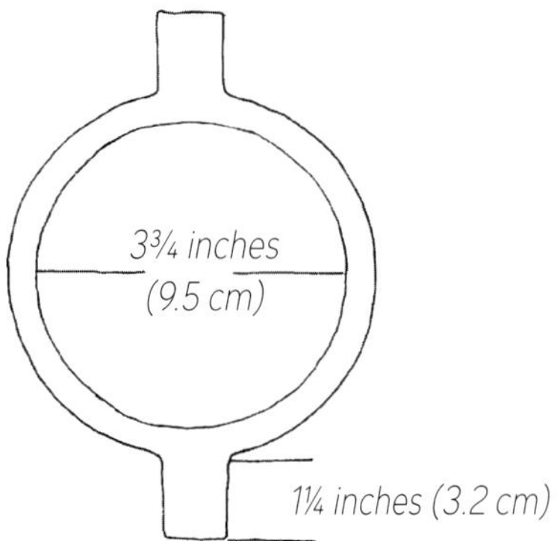

   Determining the overall thickness and width of the material is fairly arbitrary. Again, my choices are based on practical and aesthetic instinct. I decided that ¼ inch (0.6 cm) is a good thickness and 1 inch (2.5 cm) a good width. This will mean that each side of the circle is ½ inch (1.3 cm) wide.

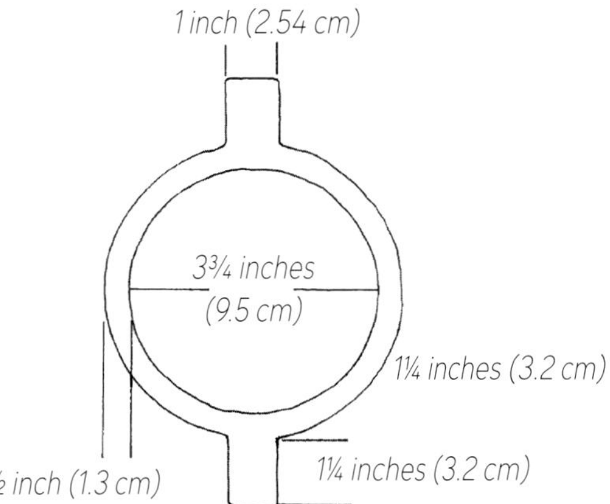

   If you wanted the tabs to be thinner and the circle to be thicker, you would need material that is as big as the thickest dimension. Figuring out the length would require you to calculate the mass of each part of the shape, convert those masses to lengths, then add those lengths together. This is a technique that blacksmiths refer to as "mass calculation." It offers exciting possibilities for forging complex shapes, but it is beyond the scope of this book, so you can look forward to learning it later.

2. Determine the length of material needed to reach the desired end shape.

   In order to do that, I imagine the final shape stretched out with the circle closed, and fill in the dimensions I know. The missing dimension will be half the circumference of the circle.

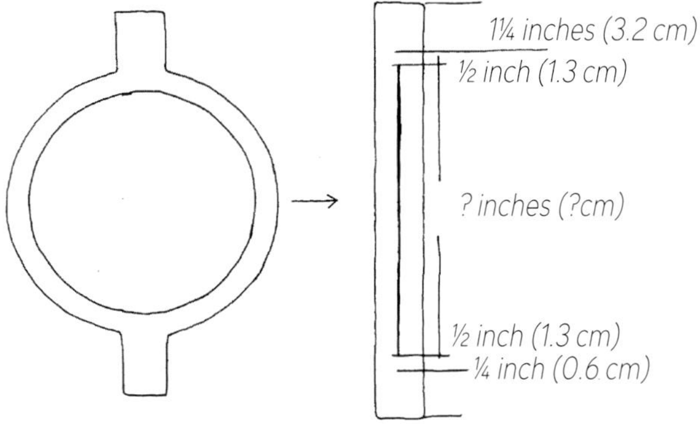

   I know the diameter is 3¾ inches (9.5 cm); using the formula C=πD (C = circumference, D = diameter), I arrive at a circumference of 11.78 inches (30 cm). I divide that in half to get 5.89 inches (14.9 cm), rounding to a final measurement of 6 inches (15 cm).

3. There's a catch! When we slit this material with the chisel so we can shape the circle, we will forge the sides of the circle, which will stretch the material, resulting in too large of a circle. We can always stretch the circle larger, but we can't shrink it smaller, so I suggest starting with a smaller measurement than calculated. Making an educated guess based on my forging experience and instinct, I reduce the middle measurement by ½ inch (1.3 cm) to arrive at 5¼ inches (13.3 cm). With that measurement, I arrive at a total length of 8¾ inches (22.2 cm).

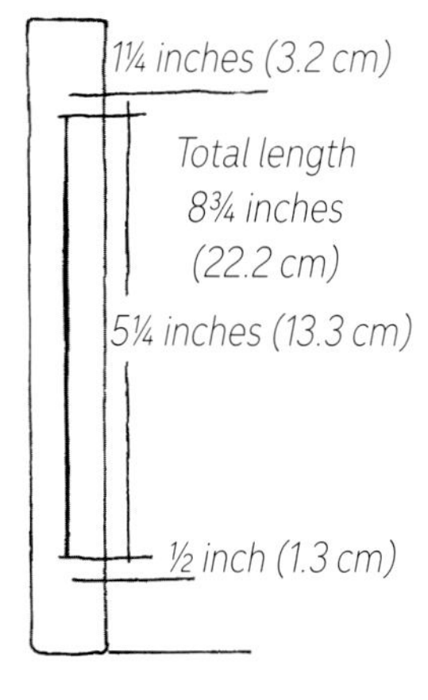

Tip: *The length of the crosspiece is determined by the size of the body piece, which is determined by the size of the pot. If you use a larger pot, you can estimate the length or wait until the body piece is finished and take your measurement directly from that. The hook lengths are fairly arbitrary, but you may want to go longer if you use a larger pot.*

1

2a

2b

HOOKS

There are three hooks in this project—two will be the same shape. The steps for these are similar to the hooks from the wall-mounted hook set (see page 144).

1. Forge ball ends on all three pieces.
2. Dimension the rest of the material to about 5⁄16 inch (0.8 cm) in diameter—just enough to fit through 3⁄8-inch (1-cm) holes.

   Now the three hooks diverge.

3. Forge a flat taper on each end of the two side hooks (the longest pieces of material). (1)
4. Bend 3 inches (7.5 cm) of these two hooks in a right angle. (2a)
5. Using the horn, form a curve in the leg of each hook, bending it around until it is parallel to the first part of the right-angle bend. (2b)

   For the middle hook pick back up here after stopping at step 2

6. Bend about 3 inches (7.5 cm) of the straight end down in a right angle.

7. Curve the material you just bent over the horn. (3a, 3b)

   The hooks are now complete.

CROSSPIECE

8. Mark, then punch and drift three ⅜-inch (1cm) holes in the crosspiece. (4a, 4b)

   My measurements are one hole in the middle, and one at ½ inch (1.3 cm) from each end. This example crosspiece is shorter than the body piece, so the hooks hang at a slight angle. I liked this look, but, if you want the hooks to be straight, wait to decide the length of the crosspiece until you've forged and can measure the body piece.

BODY

9. With the material cold, use your chisel to mark a 5¼-inch (13.3cm) line down the middle of the material. (5a)

3a

3b

4a

4b

5a

10. Punch and drift a hole on each end of this line.

The edge of the punch farthest away from you should be at the end of the line, so you do not lengthen the total opening. These holes will ensure that the inside of your circle is completely rounded. If you just chiseled the line, it would be difficult to fully round the inside areas where the tabs come off. As with the bottle opener, you could use a larger drift so you have a bigger radius to start with.

11. Use the chisel to split the material. (5b, 5c)

It will be difficult at first to cut a clean line, even with the material marked. Take your time to line up each new cut with the previous cut. Remember to cool your chisel after five to six blows. My process is to forge a deep line the whole length of the material, then cut all the way through at the far end and continue the cut as I move toward myself until I reach the other end.

Remember, you do not want to hammer your chisel directly into the face of your anvil. This will dull your chisel or cause pieces of it to chip off, which can be dangerous. If you have an anvil with a table, move to the table when you have almost cut through. The table should be unhardened and therefore softer than the face. Or, when you are almost through, flip the material over and cut from the back. Most of your force will go into splitting the surface of the material rather than the face of the anvil. You could also place a piece of softer metal, like copper or aluminum, over the face of your anvil and chisel into that. This is what I usually do, as seen in photo 5b.

5b

5c

12. Open the split you just made by placing it over the horn and hammering it back toward the body of the anvil. (6)

    Move back and forth from the horn to flatten on the face of the anvil.

6

13. Once you can fit the opening farther back on the horn, hammer the outside edge of the circle around the horn to clean up the inside edge and shape the circle. (7a, 7b)

    The most important area to shape first is the inside of the transition from the tab to the circle. You can forge this from the outside of the circle at the shoulder where the tab starts, but it also helps to hit the end of the tab in toward the circle to open it up. You will want to flip the piece periodically to heat and hammer from both sides. Remember, you do not want your circle to be too large for your pot. Hammer carefully so as not to stretch it too much, and check it on the pot frequently.

7a

7b

14. Continue to forge the circle until it is the right size and shape to fit the pot. (8)

15. Punch a hole in each tab, and you have finished the body piece. (9)

PUTTING THE PIECES TOGETHER

The last step is to shape the side hooks so they hold the body piece. The key to the body piece hanging flat, so the pot isn't tipped, is for the hooks to support it via the tabs.

16. If you fully shaped the ends of the hooks first, they would not fit through the holes of the crosspiece or body, so you have to finish the hooks with them threaded through. (10)

    If you have a small clamp of some kind, it may help to hold the crosspiece and body together to keep them out of your way as you finish the hooks.

17. With the hooks through the holes, curve the very end of each hook up so it meets the other side of the vertical part of the hook. (11)

    The goal is to have an oval on the end of each vertical piece. The top flat parts of the oval should be perpendicular to the vertical part, so they keep the body piece flat. You also want the hooks to be the same length, so the pot hangs horizontally. There will be lots of fiddling with the pieces together to achieve the goal. Think about where the metal needs to be adjusted and what tools you have to move it where it needs to be. This is the fun, problem-solving, figure-it-out-yourself part!

18. Thread the middle hook through the crosspiece and adjust all pieces until you are satisfied, and you are done. (12)

8

11

9

12

10

Glossary of Terms

alloy steel—Steels with a larger percentage of alloying elements than carbon steels.

anneal—A specific step in a heat-treating process that is meant to make the metal as soft and flexible as possible.

bic—The pointy cylindrical end of an anvil (also called a horn).

brazing—Joining pieces of metal by heating them and adding a filler material that melts into the joint.

carbon steel—*see* mild steel.

center punch—A small tool that is sharpened to a point at one end and hammered at the other end. It is used to mark metal for drilling and other purposes.

draw out—To thin and lengthen material.

dressed/dressing—The process of grinding, sanding, sharpening, and/or polishing a tool.

drift—A tool that is hammered through a piece of metal to stretch a hole to the desired size and shape. Usually used in conjunction with a punch.

face of an anvil—The flat surface of an anvil on which hammering occurs.

ferrous—Iron-based magnetic metal.

finial—The decorative end of a piece of metal. It can be any shape.

fire brick—A brick-shaped piece of ceramic-type material that will not crack or melt when heated.

fuller—A family of tools that are placed on top of hot metal and hammered into the metal to shape it.

fullering—The act of shaping metal with a fuller tool.

hardy—A family of tools, typically a type that fits into the hardy hole of an anvil, but sometimes simply a tool that a piece of hot metal is set on top of and hammered into to shape it.

hardy hole—A square hole through the top of an anvil, usually toward the back edge of the anvil.

heat/heats—One heat is one placement on the workpiece in the forge until it is the proper heat.

heat treat—A general term for controlled heating and cooling of metal to achieve the desired balance of hardness and flexibility.

heel of an anvil—Thinnest part of the anvil on the end opposite the horn.

horn—The pointy cylindrical end of an anvil (also called a bic).

inside diameter (ID)—A measurement of the diameter of the inside of a round piece of pipe or tubing.

joinery—The various methods and techniques by which multiple pieces of metal are connected.

kerf—the width of the cut or groove created by a saw or other cutting tool. It represents the material that is removed during the cutting process.

mild steel—The most common form of steel, a simple alloy of iron and carbon (also called carbon steel).

neutral flame—The result of burning gases in the correct proportion for ideal combustion.

nonferrous—Non-iron-based, nonmagnetic metal.

outside diameter (OD)—A measurement of the diameter of the outside of a round piece of pipe or tubing.

Pritchel hole—A small round hole through the top of an anvil, usually at the back corner, through the thinnest part of the anvil.

punch—A tool that is sharp at one end and is hammered into a piece of metal to make a hole.

quench—To cool metal rapidly, usually in water but sometimes in oil or other liquids.

reins—The handles on a pair of tongs.

rivet—A metal pin that is hammered on both ends to permanently connect multiple pieces of metal.

Acknowledgments

This book would not exist without the support of my partner, Chris, and the tolerance of my toddler, Brenna. Chris and I meeting was one of the great events in the history of the cosmos, second only to the Big Bang. Brenna is the absolute monarch of my heart and soul, and I humbly accept her royal dispensation for this endeavor. I started writing this while I was nursing her and am finishing just before the arrival of our baby boy, who I can't wait to meet!

Many thanks always for the best parts of myself to my mom and dad. With special gratitude to my mom for her dedication to my education by homeschooling me through high school. I am still surprised that my parents supported my pursuit of an art degree, and I can never thank them enough for their nurturing of my creativity. My four siblings, Jasmine, Jubilee, Jordyn, and Joshua, are my friends and companions for life. They inspire me with their own creative endeavors and make me want to be the best version of myself.

Dan and Andy Patterson of Santa Barbara Forge and Iron introduced me to blacksmithing. They let a weird art student hang out at their business as an apprentice, and took the time to teach her. No amount of thanks could equal that opportunity. Andy was my first blacksmithing teacher, which is a gift I can never repay. Kyle Luker, a far more competent employee than I ever was, is to blame for teaching me welding, and he continues to get me out of trouble by answering my GTAW-related questions.

I thank Jeffrey Funk at the New Agrarian School for the opportunities he has extended to me as a student and an instructor. He is one of the very best blacksmiths—not to mention people—that I know, and I learn more in a day around him than a year of working by myself.

A multitude of thanks to Margo Alleman, my friend, shopmate, coworker, collaborator. They read multiple versions of this text, offered helpful input and editing, and provided advice and expertise that made this book what it is.

More thanks than I can count goes to Rachel David, Lisa Geertsen, and Anne Bujold—all current or former members of the Governance Committee for the Society of Inclusive Blacksmiths (SIBs). Their friendships mean the world to me, and I am constantly inspired by their work and astounded by their talents. To everyone in the SIBs community, thank you for being you. Being part of a craft network full of fierce love, support, and acceptance is an irreplaceable source of strength and encouragement.

Last but by no means least, thanks to Jo Bryant and BlueRed Press for approaching me with this opportunity. I am delighted that they wanted to find a female author for this project, and extremely humbled that it ended up being me. Without Jo, this book would not exist, and I cannot thank her enough.

My deepest expressions of love and gratitude to you all.